Front endpapers:
View from the Kremlin
overlooking Moscow

Back endpapers:
Rachmaninoff in recital, Washington,
D.C., December 9, 1934 (left);
manuscript page of Piano Concerto
No. 4

RACHMANINOFF
his life and times

Sergei Rachmaninoff

RACHMANINOFF

his life and times

Robert Walker

Paganiniana Publications, Inc.
211 West Sylvania Avenue, Neptune City, N.J. 07753

To my son Paul

ISBN 0-87666-582-2

Published by PAGANINIANA PUBLICATIONS, INC.
211 West Sylvania Avenue
Neptune City, New Jersey 07753

Foreword

This book is the story of a great composer's life, told against the background of the country into which he was born, and against the times during which he lived. It has been written, therefore, with the general reader and music-lover, rather than the specialist, in mind. The popularity of Rachmaninoff's music has never fallen, but the success of two or three works tended to obscure his other achievements as a composer. It is perhaps only since the centenary in 1973 that the full achievement of this remarkable musician has been revealed to the public at large. At one time, Rachmaninoff's greatest works — the symphonies, the *Symphonic Dances*, the songs, the *Night Vigil*, the opera *The Miserly Knight* — were virtually unknown, but thanks to the dedicated work of Soviet musicians, recordings and publications of this music have been made available to all. Rachmaninoff was one of the first great musicians to pursue an extensive recording career, for nearly a quarter of a century, and these recordings, apart from being priceless historical documents, played an important part in Rachmaninoff's life. I trust the attention given to them here will set this part of Rachmaninoff's work into greater perspective.

For the courtesy, time and information given to me, I sincerely thank the late Leopold Stokowski, and Eugene Ormandy, Vladimir Horowitz, Arthur Rubinstein, Abram Chasins, Robert Simpson, Leslie Slote, Oleg Vassiliev and his colleagues in the USSR, Jack Pfeiffer, Paul Myers, David S. Levenson, Anthony Pollard, Edward Johnson, Michael Scott, John Snashall, Bryan Crimp, R. Temple Savage, Jim Fuller, Hilary C. Thomson, Peter Wadland, Christopher Ford and Denis Hall. My thanks are also due to those organisations who have kindly permitted the use of copyright photographs and material.

In transliterating Russian names into English, no attempt has been made to be completely consistent: I have used those forms most familiar to English-speaking people, and where alternatives exist I have endeavoured to use the forms adopted by the persons concerned. At the time of Rachmaninoff's birth, the Julian calendar used in Russia was twelve days behind the Gregorian, used in the West. On January 1st, 1901 it increased to thirteen days, but came into line with the Gregorian calendar after the Revolution of 1917. Consequently, for events concerning Rachmaninoff's life which took place in Russia until that time, dates are given in both forms.

No biographical study of Rachmaninoff, however brief or however lengthy, can be undertaken without acknowledging the endeavours of previous authors in this field. The work of Bertensson and Leyda deserves pride of place, but to a greater or lesser degree I owe thanks to all who have published earlier studies of this great composer and great human being. Finally, I wish to express my deep gratitude to my wife Lynn, whose loving patience and encouragement during the writing of this book have been invaluable.

RMW
London SE12
September 1979

Contents

Sergei Rachmaninoff
1873-1943
Photo: RCA

1 Roots

The coat of arms of the Rachmaninoff family, granted to them by the daughter of Peter the Great.

Peter the Great 1672-1725

By 1873 the reign of Tsar Alexander II of Russia had entered its final decade. He succeeded his father in 1855, inheriting a discredited regime, yet by immense effort he introduced long-overdue reforms which began to transform Russia from a quasi-medieval country into a reasonably modern state.

Alexander ruled his vast country from the capital, St Petersburg, a breathtakingly beautiful city founded in 1703 by Peter the Great during the Nordic War against Charles XII of Sweden. The completion of this great capital made Russia a Baltic power, with consequential development of maritime trade. It was a different city from Moscow, the old capital, being European in style: Peter visited the West in 1697-8 and for him Western models were essential to the development of his country. With an autocratic ruler, the Russian people were no better off after Peter's death than they were before he came to the throne, and he left a legacy of absolutism which was rivalled only by Catherine the Great (1762-96). Catherine was a remarkable woman: a poorly-educated German princess, strongly influenced by the ideas of the French Enlightenment, she instituted further internal reform, and continued the expansionist policies of Peter. The people paid a heavy price: her rule, which began in the reforming spirit of a new liberalism, ended, not for the last time in Russian history, with tyranny and oppression.

Catherine's son Paul I (1796-1801) was quite unlike his mother. Possibly mentally abnormal, he was murdered in a Palace coup, and succeeded by the first of his two sons who were to reign after him, Alexander I (1801-25). Alexander had much in common with his grandmother, but events in Europe forced him into wars against Napoleon, which reached their climax in 1812. In June of that year, Napoleon invaded Russia and occupied Moscow for a time, before the great fire started by the Muscovites forced him to retreat. From that point on he was beaten. As Tolstoy graphically demonstrated in *War and Peace*, the real heroes of the 1812 victory were the Russian people themselves.

Alexander pursued Napoleon across the border and in March 1814 he entered Paris, helping to destroy, as he put it, 'this

1

The Decembrists, leaders of the revolt in December 1825.

Many composers have been inspired by the work of Russia's greatest Romantic poet, Alexander Pushkin.

abomination'. For the first time Russia became a leading voice in European affairs, during the subsequent negotiations at the Congress of Vienna. The French campaign opened up a great influx of European ideas into Russia. Pushkin was caught in this excitement, and his *Ruslan and Ludmila* not only later inspired Glinka's opera (1842), but was begun at a time — 1817 — when a new Russian self-awareness was beginning to manifest itself. It was in 1817 that the Irish composer and pianist John Field, then living in Russia, gave piano lessons to the 13-year-old Glinka. He also numbered among his pupils Arkady Rachmaninoff, an ex-Army officer and enthusiastic musician, who doubtless later met both Pushkin and Glinka at the home of their mutual friend Count Vielgorsky.

The death of Alexander I in 1825 threw Russia into a political turmoil. He died childless, and the throne should have passed to his brother Constantine. But Constantine had secretly decided three years before to renounce the throne, which then passed to his younger brother Nicholas. However, Nicholas, unaware of the decree which Constantine had signed, swore allegiance to his brother, and the confusion which followed gave additional impetus to a small dissident faction opposed to Alexander's autocratic government.

Some army units, confused at the disorder in the Palace, refused to take the new oath of allegiance to Nicholas. As a result, fighting broke out in the morning of December 26th in the Square outside the Senate House. Night comes early in the Russian Winter, and by mid-afternoon it was already dark. In the gloom Nicholas himself gave the order to open fire on his own troops, and by five o'clock the insurrection was over. Not many were killed, but the incident was enough to light the fuse of the Revolution which smouldered intermittently until it exploded in 1917. 'The Decembrists', as they were called, became honoured martyrs in Soviet Russian history.

The reign of Nicholas I thus began in bloodshed. Unlike his brother Alexander, he saw the re-imposition of autocratic dictatorship as the only way of dealing with the liberal ideas flooding in

2

Mikhail Ivanovich
Glinka, 1804-1857

from the West. Totally out of touch with contemporary thought he formed a powerful secret police. His insular view, doubtless conditioned by the immense cost of the Napoleonic wars, resulted in fiercely reactionary oppression. Many opponents were arrested or forced to live abroad where they came to be influenced by the writings of Marx and Engels. These émigrés came to play an important part in Russian history.

These events did little to disturb the life of Arkady Rachmaninoff, the soldier-pupil of John Field. He had married successfully, and his nine children were well looked-after on his large estate at Znamenskoe. Music played a natural part in his family's life, for Arkady's father Alexander had formed a small orchestra in the adjoining town.

A frequent guest, Princess Golizin, whose father's estate was close to that of Znamenskoe, recalled the atmosphere of the Rachmaninoff mansion:

> We used to wake up to the accompaniment of . . . Chopin, Field or Mendelsohn's music, for Arkady Rachmaninoff went straight to the piano as soon as he got up . . . After tea in the afternoon, [he] took his place at the piano, and, striking a few chords from the song he wanted me to sing, would ask me to join him. These *musicales* usually began with an aria from *Ruslan and Ludmila* . . .

With his military experience and comfortable circumstances, Arkady was able to temper his artistic dreams and to shelter his family from the outside world. However, he was anxious to ensure his sons did not remain inexperienced in worldly matters and when one of them, Vasily, volunteered for the Army at the age of 16, Arkady did nothing to stop him.

Vasily's youthful ardour was inspired by the Crimean War, which was largely the result of Nicholas I being carried away by his own vanity. Nicholas's authoritarian regime had borne results. Russia was certainly forged into a formidable whole, and, when confronted by what he termed as "the sick man of Europe",

A bastion at Sevastopol
(*Moscow State Museum*).

3

Turkey, Nicholas thought he could easily expand his Empire. It was a bad mistake: England, France and Italy joined a Western alliance against Russia, together with Austria. The Western powers, unable to attack Russia directly, attacked where they could and consequently the land fighting was confined to Crimea where the siege of Sevastopol became the turning-point in the conflict. It lasted 350 days, during which time Nicholas died a broken man, defeated both by his inflexibility and by his imagined invincibility of the now bankrupt regime.

The Crimean War marked a turning-point in European history. The way was clear for the new Tsar, Alexander II, to bring peace and much-needed reform to his country. The war proved that Russia could be beaten, and it drove a rift between Russia and Austria which eventually became one of the major causes of the First World War. Internally, however, discontent became rife. For Russia to be defeated on Russian soil was a great humiliation. However, the Western powers did not press home their success at Sevastopol, neither did Austria attack Russia. So when Alexander concluded the Peace of Paris on March 30th, 1856, the limitations imposed on Russia were few. The discontent inside Russia, made worse by the muddles of the Crimean War, was seized upon by several of her neighbours who saw an opportunity to harass Russia on the borders. Among these was the Caucasian leader Chamyl who, in the hills of Dagestan, fought a running battle with the Russian army during the years 1857-9. It was to this campaign that the newly-trained young officer, Vasily Rachmaninoff, was sent. Chamyl was defeated, the Russian Empire grew larger, and the victorious troops came home.

Apart from military duties, a Russian army officer was required to participate in a full social life. Drinking, gambling and almost all other forms of licentiousness were common, and Vasily was drawn into the social conventions of his fellow-officers. He was not alone: in 1856, the 17-year-old Mussorgsky joined the Preobajensky Guards, where he quickly met Alexander Borodin, a 23-year-old doctor on the staff of the St Petersburg military hospital. The demanding social habits soon took hold of Mussorgsky — the chronic alcoholism, which killed him in 1881, began here.

For Vasily Rachmaninoff the social requirements of military life were also damaging. He acquired the reputation of being a ladies' man and a gambler. He was no criminal but his efforts to impress his fellow-officers were the seeds of his own downfall, like that of Mussorgsky. Vasily's military career had its compensations for he met the family of General Peter Boutakov and, following his departure from the army and his return to civilian life when his commission expired, he eventually married the General's daughter, Lubov. She had had a very different upbringing from her husband.

During 1861 Alexander signed the Decree which abolished serfdom in Russia. That at least was his intention. But many land-owners were loth to give up virtual slave-labour, and the effective-ness of the Decree was not complete as the peasants were obliged to

Modest Petrovitch
Mussorgsky, 1839-1881
(Portrait by Repin).

4

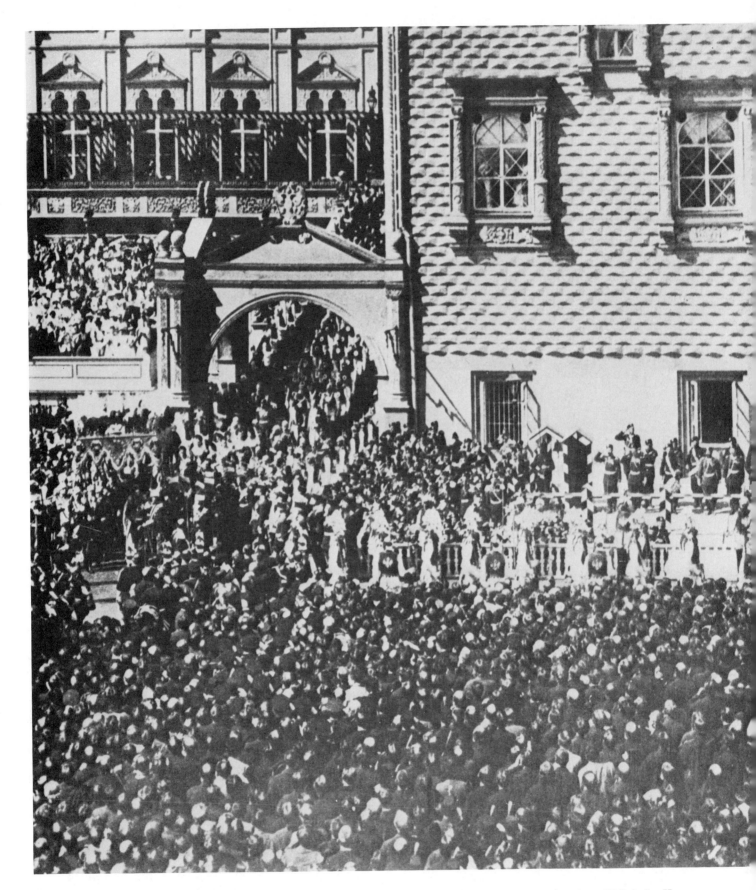

The coronation procession of Nicholas II

John Field (1782-1837)

Alexander Porphyrevitch
Borodin, 1833-1887.

Mily Alexeivitch
Balakirev, 1837-1910
(Drawing by Léon Bakst).

remain in their villages. Though they were no longer their master's property their emancipation made them liable for taxes, so that many peasants were actually worse off than before.

For reactionaries the Decree went too far: for reformers it did not go far enough. But taken with Alexander's other reforms — those of the courts, the army, the civil service, and the curtailment of the secret police — his early years as Tsar were in marked contrast to his father's reign.

The influx of European thinking during the reigns of Alexander I and Alexander II was not confined to politics. Culturally, Russia gradually came under European influence, causing serious artistic difficulties, which are best illustrated by the musical climate of the time. Until 1862, when the St Petersburg Conservatory was founded, there had not been a music college in Russia. Apart from the visits of foreign music teachers such as John Field, any Russian wishing to study music seriously had to do so in Europe, especially in Germany. This was reasonable enough up to a point; but it meant the essential features of Russian music tended to be suffocated by the influence of Germanic teaching. Anton Rubinstein, for example, born in 1829 at Podolia close to the Rumanian border, had to travel to Berlin to study composition, and those few compositions of his which are heard today could hardly be described as Russian at all. Glinka had also gained much of his early training in Berlin with the same man who, twenty-five years later, also taught Anton Rubinstein. For those younger musicians of the mid-nineteenth-century, caught up in the ferment of intellectual liberalism, this Germanic influence was as insufferable as the political restraints of Nicholas's rule. So when the St Petersburg Conservatory of Music was founded by Anton Rubinstein in 1862 it was immediately attacked by a group of younger composers for being too cosmopolitan. This group was led by the brilliant Mily Balakirev, and included the ex-military comrades Mussorgsky and Borodin. Balakirev was a disciple of Glinka, the recent commercial failure of whose opera *Ruslan and Ludmila* led Rubinstein to comment that nationalism in music was a doomed artistic quality.

Rubinstein was mistaken in not appointing a single Russian among the first professors at the St Petersburg Conservatory, for musical teaching in Russia before 1862 had not been non-existent. John Field exerted enormous influence, and among his pupils, apart from Arkady Rachmaninoff and Glinka, was Alexander Dubuque, who became a highly-regarded piano teacher in Moscow. Among Dubuque's pupils were Nikolai Zverev and Anton Rubinstein, as well as the latter's younger brother, Nicholas. Balakirev also took lessons with Dubuque, so a large part of the Russian school of pianism stemmed directly from John Field. To younger musicians, anxious to study rather than become embroiled in pseudo-political rows, the opening of the conservatory was a godsend. Among its first pupils was Peter Tchaikovsky, then in his early twenties.

5

Madame Boutakova, the maternal grandmother of Rachmaninoff.

For the Rachmaninoff family these were times of change as well. Arkady was seeing his large family grow up: Vasily had served in the army, and one of Arkady's daughters Julia, a music-lover like her father, married the young Siloti in 1862. Their son Alexander was born on October 10th the following year. Although Arkady was affected by the Decree of 1861, such information as can be gleaned from descriptions of life at Znamenskoe leads one to believe he was no tyrant. The name Rachmaninoff stems from the root *rachmany* which, in the Moscow and Tver districts, meant 'hospitable' or 'generous', and these characteristics, so touchingly described by Princess Golizin, endeared him to his family and his servants.

General Peter Boutakov was doubtless well pleased to give his blessing to the marriage of his only daughter Lubov to the young ex-army officer Vasily Rachmaninoff. The Rachmaninoffs were wealthy, well-respected and had a strong military tradition. Lubov brought five estates as her dowry, and the young couple made one of them, Oneg, their main home. This was in the Novgorod district about twenty miles from Novgorod itself, almost one hundred miles south-west of St Petersburg. At first their marriage appeared happy enough: two daughters, Elena and Sophia, began their family, and their first son, Vladimir, was born soon afterwards.

The musical life of Russia was growing, too. The success of the St Petersburg Conservatory led to the founding of a similar faculty in Moscow, in 1866, by Nicholas Rubinstein, Anton's younger brother. The first professor appointed by Nicholas was the 26-year-old Tchaikovsky, a recent graduate of the St Petersburg Conservatory. Another founder-member of the faculty was the Rubinstein brother's fellow-pupil of Alexander Dubuque, Nikolai Zverev. In terms of teaching standards, therefore, the new conservatory at Moscow was no different from that at St Petersburg, and the nationalist group of 'The Five'[1] (Balakirev, Mussorgsky, Borodin, Rimsky-Korsakov and Cui) had further cause for complaint. The two conservatories became rivals in terms of civic pride: the traditional faction, the Muscovites, who always resented the usurping of Moscow as the old capital when St Petersburg was built, now had another weapon to set against the capital. By this time, however, the anti-establishment teachings of Balakirev and his followers were losing their force. Balakirev weakened under the strain of fighting the conservatories and the financial collapse of his own Free Music School, set up in opposition to Anton Rubinstein's St Petersburg Conservatory. This institution was free in both senses: the pupils paid nothing, and the teaching was haphazard. By 1870 it was too much for Balakirev: he threw it all up and took a job on the railways in Warsaw, in the freight department.

The unification of Germany in 1870, and the German invasion of France, spurred Alexander II to reform the Russian army, in which he took a strong interest. A St Petersburg gunsmith

[1] Although known as such, their nickname is more properly translated as 'The Mighty Handful'.

The composer's parents, Vasily and Lubov Rachmaninoff.

Gershovitz reported that he had invented a new automatic weapon which Alexander II much admired, and the Tsar bought the rights from the inventor. Gershovitz was doubly happy as his wife had given birth to a son, Morris, early in 1871.

By the summer of 1872, Lubov was beginning to doubt the wisdom of her marriage to Vasily Rachmaninoff. Vasily, although inheriting some of Arkady's characteristics, had evidently not inherited them all. He spent money quickly, and a lot of it, mainly on frivolous things. Another meaning of *rachmany* is 'spendthrift', and however lovable a rogue Vasily had become, he was still a rogue: he was forced to sell the estates, one by one, to pay for his scatter-brained pursuits.

In that same summer of 1872, Lubov again became pregnant. Vasily's exploits now meant that four of their five estates had been sold, leaving only Oneg remaining. With their fourth child due at the end of March there would be further demands on their resources. Their new baby, a second son, Sergei, was born at Oneg on March 20/April 2, 1873, and his birth was registered in the church of the village of Semeonovo a few miles from the estate.

2 Childhood

For Lubov and Vasily life began anew at Oneg. By most standards they were comparatively well-off. Their last remaining estate was comfortable and, if Vasily had learned the lessons of his profligacy, they could have enjoyed a happy life. It was not to be.

Two further children were born to them: Varvara, who died when still a baby, and their last child, a third son, Arkady. For the rest of the decade their life was stable: Vasily restrained his former ways, and Oneg remained in his ownership. For the Buskin family, successful furriers in St Petersburg, it was also a happy time: their daughter, Rose, was born.

For the time being the Rachmaninoffs were reasonably secure. Lubov had her hands full with the children and when she wanted to punish them she made them sit under the piano. In later life Rachmaninoff remembered this distinctly, and his mother, a proficient pianist, encouraged Sergei's musical bias. Lubov and Vasily would have heard with interest of the success of their nephew, Alexander Siloti, who had become a pupil of Nikolai Zverev at the Moscow Conservatory. Siloti attended the disastrous première of Tchaikovsky's *Swan Lake* in 1877, the year in which the American inventor Thomas Alva Edison patented his talking machine, the phonograph, soon to be known outside the U.S.A. as the gramophone.

Alexander Siloti's success as Zverev's pupil probably spurred the Rachmaninoffs to encourage Sergei's natural love of music. When he was six, they engaged Anna Ornatskaya, a graduate of the St Petersburg Conservatory, to give him piano lessons. During his grandfather's last visit to Oneg, Sergei joined with old Arkady in improvised duets. One wonders what went through the old man's mind as he sat next to his grandson. Perhaps he remembered his own lessons with John Field, sixty years before, or maybe he pondered the implications of a new war, which Alexander II declared against Turkey in 1877.

The implications were entirely political: the nationalist movement overstepped its mark, and forced Germany to join Austria in an alliance in 1879. The seeds of future war between Russia and the Austrian-German axis were sown, and internal opposition to

An early study of the
composer in the 1880's.

reactionary policies grew. A revolutionary society, called 'Land and
Liberty' clandestinely condemned Alexander II to death in August
1879, and during the next twelve months he survived no fewer than
four assassination attempts.

Through all this unrest and personal danger, Alexander II
continued with his reforms, although without the enthusiasm
which marked the beginning of his reign. His Silver Jubilee in 1880
was celebrated in suitable style and Borodin was one of several
composers commissioned to write for the occasion. The result was
In the Steppes of Central Asia, first performed on April 8th/21st,
conducted by Rimsky-Korsakov. However, the terrorists meant
business: 'The People's Will', the guerilla faction of the 'Land and

Tsar Alexander II.

Liberty' society, planned an attack. Two revolutionaries pretending to be a married couple rented a cheese shop in a street where the Tsar frequently rode in his carriage. Working from the cellar of the shop they dug out under the street and laid a mine in the middle of the road. In case the route was changed, four further terrorists agreed to throw bombs. The route was indeed changed, on March 13th/26th 1881, and two bombs were thrown. The first killed a soldier and a butcher's boy who was watching the procession. The Tsar was unhurt, but his carriage was damaged. He was about to mount another carriage when the second bomb was thrown: he was mortally wounded, and died several hours later. Earlier the same day he had signed a Decree approving the formation of a democratically-elected, law-making parliament.

In the Nikolaevsky Military Hospital in the suburbs of St Petersburg, Mussorgsky had just been discharged following a pathetic attack induced by his chronic alcoholism. His friend, the painter Ilya Repin, was able to dry him out long enough to paint the last portrait of the composer, full of haunting dread and dissolution. Ten days later, on March 16th/29th, Mussorgsky was dead, one week after his forty-second birthday.

10

For Vasily Rachmaninoff these were trying times. Once again he had failed to control his affairs and towards the end of 1881 it became clear that Oneg would have to be sold, and the family reduced to penury. The long, happy days on the beautiful estate were at an end, and they were obliged to move to St Petersburg where the residue from the sale of Oneg was enough to buy a small flat. Vladimir, the eldest son, lived away from home during the week, attending a military academy. Sergei, on the recommendation of his teacher Anna Ornatskaya, obtained a scholarship to the St Petersburg Conservatory. He also lived away from home for several weeks with his Aunt Maria Trubnikova. Later, Sergei studied with Anna Ornatskaya's former teacher, Gustav Cross, but first fate dealt the family a tragic blow. No sooner had they settled in their small flat than a diphtheria epidemic struck St Petersburg: Vladimir, Sergei and their second eldest sister, Sophia, all went down with it. Vladimir and Sergei recovered, but Sophia died. Relations between Vasily and his wife now reached rock-bottom. In Lubov's eyes, Vasily had much to answer for: her daughter would still be alive had they remained safely at Oneg, and to have seen their circumstances descend from comparative affluence to near-poverty in almost twenty years was insufferable. For Vasily, the humiliation of the results of his recklessness was too much: he abandoned his family, left the city, and never saw his wife again.

In this black situation, Lubov showed her strength of character. She was virtually penniless, with three boys and a girl to bring up. Divorce was impossible (although not actually forbidden, the laws of the Russian Orthodox Church made it extremely difficult), and Vasily had nothing. The education of two boys seemed secure: Vladimir was at the academy, his fees paid out of public funds, and Sergei had his scholarship to the Conservatory. She turned to her mother for help. Madame Boutakova readily responded: she visited them frequently, travelling up from her home in Novgorod. Sergei was her favourite, and to console the children she bought a small farm at Borivoso, near Novgorod, where they spent some happy times not very different from the life they enjoyed at Oneg.

In London on April 18th 1882, a son was born to the Irish wife of a Polish émigré cabinet-maker who had left his country to escape the harsh rule of Russian domination. The baby was named Leopold Anthony Stokowski.

In Russia, Alexander III had quickly assumed the government. Just as his father differed from Nicholas II, so the new Tsar adopted a very changed course from that of *his* father. The assassination put an end to liberal reform and young revolutionaries were hunted down by the newly-strengthened secret police. An early example of the repressiveness of the new regime was the *diktat* in 1882 compelling Jews to confine themselves to fifteen selected provinces. Many left Russia as a result.

During a visit to Paris in March 1881, Nicholas Rubinstein had died suddenly, and the following year the directors of the Moscow section of the Russian Imperial Musical Society decided to fund a

11

A view of St. Petersburg in the 1880's taken from Vasilevski Island.

scholarship in his memory, to enable the most brilliant graduates to study abroad. Sergei's cousin, Alexander Siloti, on Zverev's recommendation had been awarded the first scholarship. He travelled first to Leipzig for the music festival of the *Allgemeine Deutsche Musikverein,* where he met the great pianist and composer with whom he was to study — Franz Liszt. Later, in Weimar, the lessons continued at Liszt's home for many months.

However brilliantly Alexander Siloti's career was developing, in the Rachmaninoff household Sergei revelled in a new freedom. Without a father-figure to exert a restraining hand (although it is doubtful if Vasily would have been a good influence, had he stayed), Sergei gave more time to games and indolence than was good for him. He frequently played truant, spending the ten kopecks for his car-fare on amusements in the skating-rink, or swimming, or playing a dangerous 'chicken' game with other boys of jumping on and off fast-moving trams.

For three years Sergei enjoyed this idyllic existence: truancy from school, fun and games in the city, and blissful holidays at Borivoso

12

Franz Liszt (1811-1866)

Alexander Siloti with Peter Tchaikovsky

A tower of the Kremlin overlooking the Moscow River

whenever the occasion arose. He accompanied his grandmother to Orthodox Church services where the choral singing and sound of the church bells greatly impressed him.

He was not the only child in his family to show musical gifts: during their time at St Petersburg, his elder sister Elena developed her outstanding contralto voice to the point where she considered a musical career. In later life Rachmaninoff recalled her with deep affection, for it was she who first introduced him to the music of Tchaikovsky. Tchaikovsky's song, "None but the Lonely Heart", is one that Rachmaninoff particularly remembered. He said Elena often accompanied herself on the piano, although when he played for her he cared less for the vocal line than the piano part.

At the Conservatory, on those days he did attend, his progress was unremarkable: his lack of application meant matters were coming to a head. In his term reports he was able to forge marks, sometimes turning a '1' into a '4' by adding a stroke to the figure (the marks ran upwards from one to five). His mother had little knowledge of his duplicity, but by the spring of 1885 the game was up. He failed all subjects and was threatened with expulsion.

To Lubov, apart from the waste of Sergei's talents which such a course meant, it also entailed finding a place at another school, which would be difficult. She turned to someone who might possibly help: her nephew Alexander Siloti who, now 21, had returned from his studies with Liszt and had begun to make his name as a pianist. Siloti started by enquiring at the Conservatory, but the Director, Davidov, had such a low opinion of the boy that Siloti was uncertain whether or not to hear him. Fortunately he relented and recognised Sergei's talent. To Siloti, there was only one answer: the tomfoolery must stop and the boy subjected to firm discipline and study. The man to do it was Nikolai Zverev, his old teacher at the Moscow Conservatory.

On Siloti's recommendation Zverev agreed to accept Rachmaninoff as a pupil in the autumn of 1885. This meant the end of Rachmaninoff's carefree youth, separation from his family, and a move to a strange city. He was cheered by the knowledge that Elena would also be in Moscow, for after study with the St Petersburg voice-trainer Ippolit Pryanishnikov she had successfully auditioned for the Bolshoi Opera in Moscow.

Sergei spent his last summer holiday at Borivoso and Elena holidayed at the country home of their Uncle Gregor Pribïtkov in Voronezh. Just before she was to leave Elena contracted pernicious anaemia and died. She was seventeen.

Sergei was heartbroken: not only had he lost his dear sister on the threshold of what might have been a great career, but he would also be even more lonely in Moscow. Sergei was twelve years old when he left Borivoso, kissed his grandmother good-bye and, carefully protecting the hundred roubles she had sewn into the lining of his gray jacket, caught the train for Moscow. His childhood had finally come to an end: now he was on his own.

13

3   Conservatory Studies

As the train pulled into the Kursk and Nizhni-Novgorod Station in the centre of Moscow, two miles East of the Kremlin, the city must have appeared to Sergei a very different place from St Petersburg. There to meet him was his aunt Julia, Alexander's mother, for his first few days in Moscow were to be spent at her home.

The sights and activity in the ill-paved streets of Moscow crowded in on his mind, with little time for regret. It was all too new, too different, too interesting a place for a young boy to mope, but no sooner had he arrived than he was taken to Nikolai Zverev, at whose apartment on Ruzheyni Pereulok he was to stay.

At the time of Sergei's first studies with him, Zverev was 53, but looked older. His apartment was large and he shared it with his sister Anna. The pupils who studied with Zverev lived in but there were never more than three at a time. They were chosen from the elite of the Conservatory pupils, not necessarily because they came from rich families: those pupils of Zverev who were from poor circumstances were taught and maintained by him free. His income came from those families who could afford to pay, and from his Conservatory fees.

To Sergei, at home in a easy-going atmosphere, it must have seemed like a prison. He shared a large bedroom with the two other young pupils, Mikhail Pressman and Leonid Maksimov. The three boys shared two grand pianos and, apart from their lessons at the Conservatory, they each had to practise for three hours daily in the apartment. Although Zverev was frequently out, either at the Conservatory or visiting his many private pupils, often until ten in the evening, his sister Anna made sure the boys were kept hard at it. Practice began at six a.m. so they had to rise earlier. Zverev frequently enquired from the professors at the Conservatory as to his pupils progress in other subjects, and woe betide them if they had been slack.

Zverev's authority over his pupils did not end there. He was concerned that they should also acquire the airs and graces of dignified living. After they had successfully completed their initial terms at the apartment Zverev ensured that they attended the latest plays, concerts, opera, and on occasion, the better restaurants. To Zverev,

14

Anton Rubinstein (1829-1894), one of whose pupils was Tchaikovsky, was a renowned virtuoso pianist. In this painting by L. Pasternak, Tolstoy can be clearly recognised among the circle of admirers.

the social graces were an important part of his pupils' education, and the visits made a welcome respite for the boys from the rigours at home. In addition to this care for the boys' social education, Zverev frequently entertained important musicians and visiting artists at home. The boys were sometimes invited to these dinner parties, and after dinner they were required to play the piano for the distinguished guests. Apart from the experience these occasions afforded the boys of playing before an audience, the opportunity of meeting a whole succession of great artists, in a relaxed and pleasant setting, was invaluable. In no other way could Sergei have met such famous musicians as old Dubuque (who doubtless regaled the boys with stories of his meeting with Beethoven in 1823), Anton and Nicholas Rubinstein, the Tchaikovsky brothers (Peter and Modest), and his cousin Alexander who was already an important musician.

This was the world into which Sergei had been thrown. It says much for his inner strength of character that he adapted to it very quickly, with a dramatic improvement in his piano technique, so much so that when Anton Rubinstein visited Moscow to conduct the hundredth performance of his opera, *The Demon*, and heard a recital by the most outstanding Conservatory pupils, both Rachmaninoff (who was then in his first year with Zverev) and Josef Lhévinne (another highly gifted student, who did not lodge with Zverev) played for him: Sergei's piece was Bach's A minor English Suite.

15

Tchaikovsky received an honorary doctorate at Cambridge in 1893.

For the first year with Zverev, the boys studied only the piano. They played four-hand arrangements of orchestral and chamber music, which was the usual way, as Edison's phonograph was in its infancy, of getting to know the classics intimately. Sergei's composing instinct must have been aroused by the opportunity to study great music in detail. By the end of his first year with Zverev, Sergei's musical ability had improved almost out of all recognition. He attended Anton Rubinstein's series of "Historical Recitals" (which made an indelible impression), and in Moscow the first performance, on March 11th 1886, of a new symphony by Tchaikovsky, *Manfred*, Opus 58, given by the orchestra of the Russian Music Society conducted by Max Erdmannsdorfer. In this composition, rather more so than in the Fourth Symphony, Tchaikovsky uses a motto theme with great subtlety. It could well have made a deep impression on Sergei. The Conservatory heard reports of the first performance, in London, on May 19th, of another motto theme symphony: Saint-Saëns's Third, in C minor, dedicated to Liszt, Alexander's old teacher, conducted by Saint-Saëns himself. Liszt was touched by the dedication, but he passed away, less than three months after the première, on July 31st.

Zverev took the boys to the Crimea for the summer in May 1886, not so much for a holiday but to ensure that they studied harmony and theory with Zverev's fellow-Conservatory professor, Ladukhin, so that they would be well-prepared for the new academic year starting in the autumn. Having completed their first year concentrating exclusively on the piano, the boys would now enter the harmony class of Anton Arensky at the Conservatory, while still living at Zverev's apartment, with its additional practice and strict discipline.

During the summer Sergei, now a highly proficient pianist, started his first attempt at original composition, or rather, transcription. The score of Tchaikovsky's *Manfred* Symphony had just been published by Jurgenson, and Sergei began to make a piano-duet arrangement of the work. In many ways this was the kind of practical musicianship which the boy needed to supplement his piano lessons and the harmony course with Professor Ladukhin.

Towards the end of 1886 the transcription was completed, after the boys had returned to Moscow and joined Arensky's harmony class. Zverev arranged for Sergei and his fellow-boarder, Mikhail Pressman, to play the transcription of *Manfred* to the composer himself at the apartment. Tchaikovsky was probably impressed by the musicianship of the 13-year-old boy, who in turn must have been proud of meeting his musical idol on more equal terms. Whether we would be impressed with Sergei's effort must remain unanswered, for this first piece of original work by Rachmaninoff is lost.

The boys returned to the Crimea the following summer, 1887, and Mikhail Pressman recalled that during one of their visits Rachmaninoff composed his first original pieces:

16

. . . when we were alone, he called me to the piano and began to play. 'Do you know what this is?', he asked. 'No', I said, 'I don't'. 'And how do you like this pedal point in the bass against this chromatic progression in the upper register?'. I nodded satisfaction. 'I composed it myself', he said proudly, 'and I dedicate it to you'.

This piece, whatever it was, has apparently not survived either for Pressman's description does not fit any of Rachmaninoff's early pieces. A further reminiscence by Pressman gives another insight into the musical training of the boys. As well as issuing versions of orchestral works for piano duet, some publishers also made available transcriptions for eight hands at two pianos, and Zverev would engage a fourth pianist to join the boys for these. Sometimes it would be Madame Beloposkaya, but Pressman recalls an occasion when another Zverev pupil from the Conservatory, Semeon Samuelson, joined them to play before Taneyev, then Director of the Conservatory. Taneyev was astonished when the boys marched to the pianos to play Beethoven's Fifth Symphony — without music. Taneyev asked where the music was: according to Pressman, he almost jumped from the chair.

'They play by heart', replied Zverev calmly, his eyes looking upwards.

After the performance, with Taneyev still muttering, '. . . how is it possible? . . . to play by heart . . .', Zverev ordered an encore: the scherzo from Beethoven's 'Pastoral' Symphony.

Doubtless encouraged by Tchaikovsky's reception of the duet version of *Manfred*, and fired by the study of the score and his new lessons with Arensky, Rachmaninoff completed his first orchestral

Red Square, Moscow, as it was during Rachmaninoff's student days in the city.

work, a *Scherzo* in D minor, in February, 1887. It is likely he intended this to be part of a complete symphony, possibly using *Manfred* as a model, for there is a connection between the scherzo of Tchaikovsky's work and Rachmaninoff's piece in the light and delicate writing for woodwind and strings. However, Tchaikovsky's scherzo ends with one of his most magical codas, whereas Rachmaninoff's ends with a sudden loud chord. For a first attempt at orchestration it is remarkably assured and successful: Rachmaninoff had obviously learned much and was unafraid to commit himself to paper quickly, for the score bears the dates February 5th/18th — 21st/March 5th. Rachmaninoff never heard the work: its première took place in Moscow, under Nikolai Anosov, on November 2nd 1945. On January 29th 1887, at Lodz in Russian-dominated Poland, Arthur Rubinstein (no relation to the Rubinstein brothers) was born.

In the spring of 1887 Rachmaninoff composed a short piano piece, which was also lost. In 1934 he re-wrote it from memory, for publication in a book of recollections. The 14-year-old now felt the need for his 'Opus 1', and during the Zverev party's summer holiday in the Crimea in 1887 he probably composed the Four Piano Pieces, which remained unpublished during his life-time. Shortly after the start of the new academic year in the autumn of 1887 he wrote a set of *Three Nocturnes* for piano.

Rachmaninoff was now in his element. His own compositions, coupled with his growing proficiency as a pianist and his increasing musical knowledge, were moulding him into an excellent musician. Under the watchful eye of Zverev he made good progress in other subjects and, away from his family, he must have felt much more self-confident than when he first arrived in Moscow. For the Easter holiday in 1888 Zverev allowed him to visit another of his aunts, Vavara Satina, the wife of Alexander Satin, and the sister of his absconded father. He met his cousins one of whom, Natalia, also showed a strong musical character. Sergei, now a self-assured young man of 15, recognised a kindred spirit in Natalia and returned to the Conservatory for the final term, enrolling in the class of his cousin, Alexander Siloti, who had joined the faculty of the senior department.

It was becoming clear to his professors that Rachmaninoff possessed a genuine gift for composition and consequently he was allowed to join Taneyev's counterpoint class at the start of the new academic year, while remaining in Siloti's class, and still lodging at Zverev's. Rachmaninoff planned an opera, *Esmerelda*, based on Victor Hugo's *Notre Dame de Paris*. It remained unfinished, but the Introduction to Act I and fragments of Act III exist in a piano score dated October 17th/30th 1888. The stimulus of working under Taneyev was heightened by his fellow-pupils: among them was Alexander Scriabin, fifteen months older than Sergei, a native of Moscow and, like Rachmaninoff, an outstanding pianist. Scriabin was a member of Safonoff's class, as were Pressman and Josef Lhévinne, and he became firm friends with Rachmaninoff.

18

Victor Hugo (1802-1885)

Nikolai Zverev with his pupils in 1866 including Rachmaninoff at Zverev's left
and Scriabin in cadet uniform

Mily Balakirev (1837-1910)

Sergei Ivanovitch
Taneyev

Apart from the pupils' qualities, the class must have been stimulating owing to Taneyev himself. Rachmaninoff first met him at Zverev's, and Scriabin had studied with him privately before joining the Conservatory class. Taneyev's knowledge was legendary: a pupil of Tchaikovsky, he soon outstripped his master with the result that later it was Tchaikovsky who took lessons from him. Taneyev, a Muscovite, shared the aims of Balakirev and his followers, but disagreed with 'The Five' on the methods by which those aims were to be achieved: he insisted on a thorough musical education rather than the musical primitivism advocated by Balakirev, and his personal bearing made a great impression on his pupils. When he died suddenly in 1915 at the age of 58 Rachmaninoff wrote an obituary, describing the man:

. . . Through his personal example Taneyev taught us how to live, how to work, and even to speak, because he had his own 'Taneyev way' of speaking — concise, clear, and to the point. He only said what was necessary. This man never uttered superfluous words. He seemed to me to be the personification of 'Truth on Earth' which Pushkin's Salieri rejected . . .

In musical Russia the event of 1889 was the St Petersburg visit of Neumann's Opera Company, who performed Wagner's *Ring* under Karl Muck. The performances were attended by a noted Russian bass Feodor Stravinsky whose son, Igor, was then seven years old.

The liberating influence of his fellow-students directed Rachmaninoff towards composition, but Zverev thought differently. He trained Rachmaninoff as a pianist and he was an outstanding pupil. To dilute this great talent into composition was unacceptable to Zverev, especially when Rachmaninoff complained he could not compose because living at Zverev's apartment meant sharing the piano and workroom. Zverev took this complaint as a personal insult: a quarrel blew up, an almost inevitable consequence of the conflict between Zverev's severe manner and Rachmaninoff's adolescent assertion of independence. For a month, relations between the two smouldered but neither was willing to give way. It was clear Rachmaninoff would have to leave, and Zverev took him to the house of his Aunt Varvara Satina explaining that it was impossible for Rachmaninoff to remain at the apartment. Rachmaninoff left the following day.

Apart from the deep musical influence which Zverev exerted upon his pupils, Rachmaninoff was also influenced in other ways by the four years he spent with Zverev. People who knew both men commented on the resemblance of their manner and attitude towards people. Although Rachmaninoff was not dictatorial as Zverev was, in later life his aloof and distant manner immediately struck people on first meeting him. This doubtless stemmed from his time with Zverev and his studies with Taneyev, for it was in marked contrast to the easy-going boy he had been before he went to Moscow.

His mother, still in St Petersburg, suggested he return home and finish his courses at the Conservatory there. It was a tempting

Nicolai Zverev, the piano
teacher.

suggestion, for Rimsky-Korsakov and Anton Rubinstein were resident professors. Rachmaninoff refused: his musical training had been concentrated in Moscow, and he felt part of the rivalry between the Conservatories.

A fellow-student, Mikhail Slonov, put Rachmaninoff up for a while and then Aunt Varvara made room in her Moscow home for Sergei for several months. It was the perfect solution and, as the new academic year began, to the composition lessons with Taneyev were now added fugal studies with Arensky.

This change of environment with his own room gave him the first chance for peace and quiet, and the daily encounter with domestic feminine company, coupled with the final stages of his Conservatory studies began to unleash the music that was welling up in Rachmaninoff's mind. He wrote two pieces for string quartet (a *Romance* in G minor, and a *Scherzo* in D major), which were not performed in their quartet version until October 1945 in Moscow by the Beethoven Quartet. They were heard in another version, possibly for string orchestra, in Moscow on February 24th/March 9th 1891, conducted by Safonoff who succeeded Taneyev as Director of the Conservatory in 1889. In November Rachmaninoff began sketches for a Piano Concerto in C minor. He dedicated the string quartet pieces to Alexander Siloti and possibly the encouragement he received from his other cousins at his new home prompted his first songs, which date from the spring of 1890. These songs were preceded by a contrapuntal exercise, an unaccompanied six-part motet *Deus Meus*, doubtless calling on the deep impressions made during his frequent church visits with his grandmother. The first of the three songs. 'At the Gate of the Holy Place', dated April 29th/May 12th, he dedicated to his friend Mikhail Slonov (himself a singer), in gratitude for the practical help he gave Rachmaninoff following the break with Zverev (the words have some significance in this context). The second, 'I Will Tell You Nothing' followed two days later. The third song, 'Again You Leapt, My Heart' is not dated, but could have been written at this time.

At the end of the summer term, Rachmaninoff travelled with his relatives to their country estate at Ivanovka, in the Tambov district south-east of Moscow. They were joined by the Silotis and another family of cousins, the three Skalon sisters, Natalia, Ludmila, and Vera. The countryside on this big estate exerted a powerful influence on Rachmaninoff, who came to love the place dearly. Sergei must have been a charming guest at the house-parties during the summer holiday, and surrounded by so many attractive young musical girls, the 17-year-old came into his element. While at Ivanovka he composed a *Romance* for cello and piano dated August 6th/19th, which he dedicated to the youngest of the Skalon sisters Vera, and for all three he wrote a *Waltz* (for six hands at one piano) nine days later. During the summer he received his first commission, from Tchaikovsky's music publishers Jurgenson, to make a piano-duet transcription of Tchaikovsky's *The Sleeping*

20

Beauty ballet. Alexander Siloti had been approached to undertake the task, but because he was unable to accept he suggested the commission be given to Rachmaninoff whose work he would supervise. It was a golden opportunity for the young composer, who adored Tchaikovsky's music. Rachmaninoff's commission recalled the earlier transcription of Tchaikovsky's *Manfred*, for Rachmaninoff began an orchestral work on the same subject in October 1890, but never completed it, and what music he did write has been lost. Tchaikovsky had just met the young German musician Fritz Scheel for the first time and, later that month, Rachmaninoff composed another song 'In the Silence of the Secret Night', dated October 17th/30th, which was incorporated into the later Six Songs, Opus 4, of 1893. This song is Rachmaninoff's first to be published with an Opus number: it is dedicated, like the cello-and-piano *Romance* of two months previously, to Vera Skalon, for she became Rachmaninoff's favourite among the three sisters — rather too much so for her mother's liking especially in view of the song's text. She forbade the pair to write to each other after the holiday.

In spite of Rachmaninoff's apparent indifference towards the St Petersburg school, there is a distinct influence between the final section of Rimsky-Korsakov's Piano Concerto in C-sharp minor of 1883 and the first movement of a *new* Piano Concerto which Rachmaninoff began during the spring of 1890, in F-sharp minor.

Nor are these all of Rachmaninoff's compositions at this time. In 1890, he began three versions of Boris's monologue, *Ti otche patriarkh* (which were completed the following year), and two versions of Pimen's monologue *Escho odno posledneye skazan'ye* as well as a fragment, in two versions also, of Arbenin's monologue *Noch'provedennaya bez sna* from Lermontov's poem, *Maskarade*.

It was a busy time: he took a position as a teacher in a class for choirmasters, and visited his mother in St Petersburg for Christmas when he saw Tchaikovsky's opera, *The Queen of Spades*. His mother should have been proud of her son, but the two did not really get on: the years in Moscow had changed him from the care-free boy into a serious, somewhat aloof, young man. Possibly the real reason for his St Petersburg trip was the chance it afforded him to visit the Skalon family, particularly Vera. Early in January 1891, he returned to Moscow, to find everyone talking about the shortage of food. In 1890-91, European Russia faced a full-scale famine. Rachmaninoff's mother moved into a smaller apartment on the Fontanka in St Petersburg, and a possible source of friction was her demand that Sergei do something to help her financially. For the furriers in St Petersburg, the Bruskins, it meant there were fewer people able to afford their warm winter clothes: they decided to emigrate to the U.S.A., and in May they sold up and left, with their daughter Rose, then fifteen years old.

They were not the only Russians to go to New York that year: following the successful première of *The Queen of Spades* Tchaikovsky accepted an invitation to visit New York, doubtless

21

told of its life and vitality by Anton Rubinstein, to conduct at the opening of the new Carnegie Hall which the millionaire philanthropist Andrew Carnegie had endowed.

Rachmaninoff was not badly affected by the shortage of food: almost immediately on his return from St Petersburg he began work on a *Russian Rhapsody*, in E minor for two pianos,[1] written in only two days, January 12th-14th (25th-27th). He showed it to his friend Maksimov, who had been a fellow-Zverev pupil. But Zverev still bore Rachmaninoff a grudge and, hearing of the planned performance by these two, forbade Maksimov to participate. Rachmaninoff turned to another friend, Josef Lhévinne, and they premièred the *Rhapsody* in October that year in Moscow. In February, Rachmaninoff made his debût as a conductor. He directed the Moscow Conservatory Chorus in the first performance of the six-part motet *Deus Meus,* and later that month he heard the new version of the pieces for string quartet from 1889, when Safonoff conducted them in Moscow on February 24th/March 9th. Hearing his own music may have prompted him to take up the Concerto again, the first movement of which he completed the year before, for shortly afterwards he wrote to Natalia Skalon telling her the second movement was finished and he was hoping to write down the finale soon and spend the summer orchestrating it. In April he wrote two more songs: the first, a French setting of a poem by Edouard Pailleron, *C'était en Avril,* dated, appropriately enough, April 1st/14th, and, later in the month, "Twilight has fallen" on April 22nd/May 5th.

The following month a crisis arose at the Moscow Conservatory. Since Safonoff became director in 1889 relations between him and Alexander Siloti had become strained, and in May 1891 Siloti resigned. Quite apart from family considerations this meant Rachmaninoff had to change teachers for his final year, and this he was loth to do. With great daring he approached Safonoff and asked if he could take his final piano examinations one year early, which meant qualifying within a month. Safonoff agreed and the exceptional training and ability Rachmaninoff possessed now came into their own. He was required to prepare the first movement of a Chopin Sonata and a complete Beethoven Sonata. Much later, a fellow-pupil, Alexander Goldenweiser, recalled Rachmaninoff's talent:

... Rachmaninoff's musical gifts, even apart from his creative ability, surpassed any others I have ever met, bordering on the marvellous, like those of Mozart in his youth. The speed with which he memorised new compositions was remarkable. I remember how Siloti, with whom we were both studying at the time, told Rachmaninoff to learn the well-known Brahms *Variations and Fugue on a Theme of Handel*. This was on a Wednesday, and it was but three days later that Rachmaninoff played them like a master. It was his practice to memorise everything he heard, no matter how complicated it was ...

[1]Although the *Russian Rhapsody* begins in E minor, it ends in G major. A cadenza for the first piano suggests it could have been originally intended for piano and orchestra.

With this formidable technique Rachmaninoff knew what he was doing by making his request to Safonoff. On May 24th/June 6th he took the final piano examinations, and graduated with honours.

His exertions demanded a holiday, but instead of visiting his family in St Petersburg he accompanied Siloti to Ivanovka, where he finally completed the Piano Concerto in F sharp minor on July 6th/19th. He dedicated it to Siloti but he had to rush to finish the score. Once it was written he relaxed with a short piano piece, a *Prelude* in F, dated July 20th/August 2nd, preceding it with another song "Morning" which was also incorporated into the Opus 4 set. Rachmaninoff had had an encouraging year thus far, but he soon received a setback. The demands on his time cramming for his finals had taken their toll of his work in making the piano-duet transcription of Tchaikovsky's *Sleeping Beauty*. The composer was unhappy with much of Rachmaninoff's work and Siloti was obliged to make rather more corrections than he would have liked to pacify Tchaikovsky. Rachmaninoff's piano prelude was also later re-composed for a cellist friend, but in August he travelled to Znamenskoe to visit his father's mother, the widow of old Arkady Rachmaninoff. He may well have begun a Symphony in D minor here (the *Scherzo* of four years before was not part of this work), but while swimming in the river Matïr he contracted a feverish chill which worsened on his return to Ivanovka. By the end of September the one-movement Symphony was finished in full score. It is dated September 28th/October 11th: eight days previously he completed another piece for the Skalon sisters, a *Romance* in A major to complement the *Waltz* of the previous summer.

The fever troubled him intermittently. It delayed his return to Moscow, so he began the first term of the new year late. He moved into lodgings with his friend Slonov but shortly afterwards the fever returned with redoubled force. Rachmaninoff was moved to another house and confined to bed almost until the end of October, and even when he recovered sufficiently to get up he was not his usual self. He felt depressed but gradually improved, and by the end of the year was at work on a new orchestral piece, a symphonic poem *Prince Rostislav*. This is based on an early work of Count Alexei Tolstoy (a distant cousin of Leo). The score is dated December 9th/22nd-15th/28th and the work is dedicated to "My dear professor Anton Stepanovitch Arensky", who had earlier agreed to Rachmaninoff taking his final composition examinations one year early in 1892.

In spite of the completion and dedication of the work this, too, was never performed during Rachmaninoff's lifetime, being premièred in Moscow on November 2nd 1945, conducted by Nikolai Anosov. Hearing the work today, there seems little cause for regret: however superb a pianist Rachmaninoff had become this was not then matched by a similar talent in composition.

Arensky's agreement that he could take his finals in theory and composition one year early meant that Rachmaninoff had his work cut out: he had to submit a symphony, some vocal works and an

Rachmaninoff at the time of his graduation from the Moscow Conservatory.

opera. The one-movement Symphony was finished. It begins with a slow introduction before a flowing *Allegro moderato* forms the basis of the rest of the work in a mixture of 12/8 and 9/8 metres. His composition, following *Prince Rostislav*, continued apace: early in 1892 he completed his first *Trio Elégiaque* in G minor between January 18th/31st and January 21st/February 3rd. The first performance was given in Moscow nine days after its completion by Rachmaninoff with David Krein (violin) and Anatole Brandukov (cello). Brandukov became a friend and collaborator, for at the same concert he and Rachmaninoff also premièred the composer's Opus 2, *Two Pieces* for cello and piano, dedicated to Anatole, the first being a recomposition of the *Prelude* in F, the second entitled *Oriental Dance*. Like the Symphony, the Trio is in one movement, and little did Rachmaninoff realise how soon it would be before he wrote a second.

Another song followed, dated February 26th/March 10th, "Oh No, I Beg You, Forsake Me Not" which was incorporated into the Opus 4 songs the following year, but the most important event of the first few months was the première, on March 17th/30th, of the first movement of the Piano Concerto. This was at a student concert conducted by Safonoff, and a fellow-pupil, Mikhail Bukinik, later described the première:

... Safonoff, who ordinarily conducted the compositions of the students, would brutally and unceremoniously change anything he wished in these scores, cleaning them up and cutting parts to make them more playable. The student composers, happy to have their creative efforts performed . . . did not dare contradict Safonoff, and readily agreed to his comments and alterations. But Safonoff had a hard time with Rachmaninoff. This student not only refused categorically to accept alterations but also had the audacity to stop Safonoff (as conductor),

Anton Stepanovitch Arensky, 1861-1906 (seated centre) with three graduates from his 1892 composition class — Conus, Morozov and Rachmaninoff (right).

24

pointing out his errors in tempo and nuance. This was obviously displeasing to Safonoff, but being intelligent, he understood an author's rights, though a beginner, to make his own interpretation, and he tried to take the edge off any awkwardness. Besides, Rachmaninoff's talent as a composer was so obvious, and his quiet self-assurance made such an impression on all, that even the omnipotent Safonoff had to yield. . .

Safonoff had not been Rachmaninoff's tutor, but he was obviously as outstanding a teacher as Zverev and Siloti. Among those who passed through his hands were Lhévinne, Scriabin and Medtner. When Rachmaninoff came to the cadenza — a powerful, staggeringly brilliant and difficult section — Safonoff must have realised he was in the presence of a real composer. Although the Concerto was later extensively revised, the cadenza is virtually the same in both versions, giving us an insight into what Rachmaninoff was capable of at the age of 17.

Arensky, too, must have been pleased with his pupil's work and with his decision to let Rachmaninoff graduate early: before the première, Rachmaninoff wrote to Natalia Skalon on February 18th/March 2nd:

. . . April 15th is the important day for me. On March 15th, they will give us the subject for a one-act opera. As you can see, I shall have to compose it, write it out and orchestrate it in one month. No mean task . . .

It was not, but it was not helped by an incident at Rachmaninoff's lodgings. He was still sharing with Slonov but during his illness the previous winter he had stayed at the home of another Conservatory student, Yuri Sakhnovsky. Rachmaninoff's father, Vasily, had turned up in Moscow and appealed to his son for help. Sergei could not turn his father away, and it was through Sakhnovsky's help that Vasily was found a job and he moved in with his son and Slonov. When Rachmaninoff finally received the opera libretto, he dashed home to his lodgings impatient to begin. But his father had taken over the room containing the grand piano for the whole after-noon to entertain some acquaintances. Sergei was beside himself with frustration: he thought his father's action would thwart his plans but when the guests left, Sergei seized on the opera as if possessed. The subject was *Aleko*, fashioned by Vladimir Nemirovitch-Danchenko from Pushkin's poem *The Gypsies* (Tsïganï) which appeared in 1824. Nemirovitch-Danchenko felt it necessary to obscure the poem's real message, that of freedom for the Bessarabian gypsies from tyranny, as such a story seemed a little too close to home for the authorities who had informants in every college. The story was reduced to a crime of passion.

Rachmaninoff wrote *Aleko* at white-heat: the composition took fifteen days, between March 21st/April 3rd-April 4th/17th, but because the libretto was received late the examination was post-poned until May 7th/20th. The committee members were unanimous: Rachmaninoff was awarded the highest mark, and graduated with honours. A committee member was Zverev, who followed Rachmaninoff into the corridor, took him to one side,

25

congratulated him and gave Sergei his own gold watch as a token. The watch remained with Rachmaninoff for the rest of his life and the breach was healed.

Ten days later, the recipients of the Gold Medals were announced: Rachmaninoff was awarded the Great Gold Medal, which had only been awarded twice before in the Conservatory's history, with the title of "Free Artist". One of the previous winners was Taneyev, and Rachmaninoff's name was inscribed on the marble plaque under those of Taneyev and Koreschenko. The graduation concert took place on May 31st/June 13th, and afterwards Rachmaninoff left the Conservatory for the last time: his apprentice days were over and the nineteen-year-old composer now had to make his way in the world as a professional.

4   Triumph and Disaster

By the summer of 1892 the events of Rachmaninoff's life had combined to enable him to face the world fully equipped for the career he intended to pursue. He was confident of his own high ability and the years with Zverev and Taneyev made him calm and politely reserved in company. He also knew the social graces necessary for an artist to move in the highest circles. His early years away from home made him independent — indeed, his own father had turned to him for help. Rachmaninoff enjoyed good food, especially of the traditional Russian variety, and good wines and beer. He never drank to excess, just enough to relax and put him at ease with friends and family. His appearance belied a great sense of humour, which he shared with a close circle — his laugh was infectious, and when his normally placid face broke into a grin, and then turned to laughter, tears would well up in his eyes as he relished the joke. No one could keep a straight face when Rachmaninoff was in such good humour. His holidays at the estate of Ivanovka made him a first-class horseman. He smoked, as the custom of the day demanded, rather heavily: rarely less than twenty strong cigarettes a day, but he was in excellent physical shape by constitution — as had been shown by the diphtheria epidemic and the fever of 1891 — and by his professional training. His hands were enormous, and he possessed legendary strength. He had grown to just over six feet (just under two metres) and in addition to his physique, his mental outlook was sound. He had experienced personal loss and shown the resilience necessary to overcome depression.

The success of his graduation opera with the examining committee soon spread. News of the young composer came to the attention of a successful publisher of light music, Karl Gutheil, who was anxious to broaden his catalogue by including serious works and was looking for a young composer whose financial demands would not be great. Gutheil knew Zverev and asked his advice regarding Rachmaninoff's music. Zverev had made up his silly quarrel with the young composer and gave Gutheil an enthusiastic recommendation. Gutheil was on the point of approaching Rachmaninoff when Zverev told Sergei of his conversation with the publisher and suggested it might be better to seek the advice of an experienced composer before considering any offer Gutheil might make. Zverev made an appointment for Rachmaninoff to meet Tchaikovsky on the latter's return to Moscow. But Gutheil approached Rachmaninoff before he could see Tchaikovsky and asked Sergei to name his terms. As Rachmaninoff had no idea what terms to ask for a meeting with Tchaikovsky was more imperative than ever, and in due course they met. Tchaikovsky was delighted at Rachmaninoff's good fortune in having a publisher approach him and not, as was almost always the case, the other way about, but he shrewdly advised Rachmaninoff to get Gutheil to name his terms, which would leave Rachmaninoff with the final decision. After a series of meetings, with neither willing to commit to any sum, Gutheil offered 500 roubles as an outright purchase for three works: *Aleko*, the songs, and the *Two Pieces* for cello and piano. Had Rachmaninoff not been briefed to expect such an offer, his reaction might have given the game away. To the young composer 500 roubles was a fortune, as his only earnings at that time were 15 roubles a month from his one-and-only pupil. Both partners were pleased with the deal and time proved Gutheil to have made an excellent choice: he remained Rachmaninoff's loyal publisher until 1914, when the firm was taken over by Serge Koussevitsky's publishing house upon Gutheil's death.

Rachmaninoff spent part of the summer at the Konovalov estate, giving daily piano lessons to the son of the family, Alexander. Gutheil soon got to work, and Rachmaninoff received the proofs for the forthcoming publications there, which he corrected and returned. He was able to work on a piano score of *Aleko* (he had no time to prepare one for the examination), as Gutheil wanted to publish the opera in both piano and full score. For reasons which remain unknown, the full score was not published by Gutheil, being merely available on hire, but the piano score was quickly issued and sold well. The summer was enlivened by a visit from his mother and it was apparently through the good offices of a relative that *Aleko* was brought to the attention of the Imperial Opera, and accepted for performance the following year. This was excellent news: better than Sergei could possibly have hoped for, but it did not turn his head. He wrote to Natalia Skalon in June telling her of the proposed production, but also expressing a sanguine thought that the opera might not succeed as he knew he was an inexperienced composer and that 'first operas' usually failed.

After *Aleko* had been accepted for publication and performance, ideas for a new opera interested him. In 1892 he planned an opera on Zhukovsky's *Undine*, and he possibly mentioned this to Tchaikovsky. If he did, the older composer would have been intrigued, for he had written an opera on the same subject in 1869, but after it was rejected for performance he destroyed it in 1873. Tchaikovsky tackled the subject again with a new libretto provided by his brother Modest, but he was not inspired by it, and asked Modest to send Rachmaninoff the libretto. By a curious

The Iberian Gate in Moscow. Through the right arch the onion domes of St. Basil's Cathedral can be seen.

coincidence, Rachmaninoff had independently approached Modest Tchaikovsky through Zverev. So, if he really had wished to pursue *Undine* a libretto was ready and waiting. But this is to anticipate events, as *Aleko* was not yet produced, and much of the *Undine* affair happened after that.

Rachmaninoff returned to Moscow, staying with the Satins. After an attack of fever he composed a piano *Prelude* in C-sharp minor, which he played for the first time at an Electrical Exposition concert on September 26th/October 9th in Moscow. Rachmaninoff regarded this concert as his professional debût, and it is fitting that this event also marked the first performance of his most famous composition. The *Prelude* in C-sharp minor became his trademark and carried his name all over the world. While preparing a concert in Kharkov at the end of the year Rachmaninoff composed four companion pieces for the *Prelude*, and the complete set of five pieces were published as *Morceaux de fantasie*, Opus 3. Rachmaninoff dedicated the set to Arensky — a more fitting consecration than the *Prince Rostislav* symphonic poem the previous December.

In addition to the complete opera, orchestral excerpts from *Aleko* were scheduled for performance, and these developments encouraged Rachmaninoff to begin an extended orchestral work on gypsy themes. This was not completed until 1894 but it was planned during the summer of 1892.

The new year — 1893 — dawned full of promise for the nineteen-year-old Rachmaninoff. His concert in Kharkov augured well, and in Moscow he heard the orchestral dances from *Aleko* under Safonoff on February 19th/March 31st given with great success.

29

Gutheil agreed to take the Concerto and publish it as Opus 1 (although only a two-piano version was finally printed) and also paid 200 roubles for Opus 3. This meant Rachmaninoff received 40 roubles for each of the five pieces, including the *Prelude* in C-sharp minor. Apart from the recordings he made much later, and a two-piano version he transcribed in 1938, this was all he earned from the work that made him a household name the world over. But 200 roubles was still much-needed money for Rachmaninoff, as the famine which had ravaged the country for two years had seriously affected food supplies and prices were rising.

For Sergei, preparations for the première of *Aleko* pushed other considerations aside. The conductor was the music director of the Bolshoi himself, Ippolit Altani, who was then 47. A most experienced operatic conductor, Altani had been Director for eleven years, so Rachmaninoff's work could not have been in better hands. The principals were also very good, although their names mean little to us today. Rachmaninoff attended every rehearsal and was flattered when Tchaikovsky expressed his delight to Siloti at the dress rehearsal. The first performance on April 27th/May 10th was a triumph for the young composer. His father was present, and many other members of his family including his grandmother — Arkady's widow, then a very old lady — also attended. The most influential member of the audience was Tchaikovsky, who demonstrated his wholehearted approval by leaning out of his box, applauding vigorously. Sergei was called on to the stage to acknowledge the ovation.

The press, as usual, were more cautious. It is easy to pick holes in Rachmaninoff's score, but the virtues of *Aleko* are considerable: not least the *cavatina* (known better in English-speaking countries as "The Moon is High in the Sky" through the subsequent Chaliapin recording), and the final chorus, which is quite haunting. *Aleko* contains flaws: the scenes end abruptly and the characterisation is sketchy, but, if played for all it is worth, as on the old complete Russian recording conducted by Nikolai Golovonov, the work can still make a tremendous impact.

Tchaikovsky was right to encourage the young composer: he asked Rachmaninoff at rehearsal if he would object to having *Aleko* performed on the same evening as a new opera of his, *Iolanta*. Rachmaninoff later recalled: "He literally said — 'Would you object?' — he was 53, a famous composer — and I was only a twenty-year-old beginner!" Rachmaninoff, flushed with success, visited his grandparents General and Madame Boukatov, who must have been proud to hear of his triumph at first-hand. Afterwards, he stayed with Slonov on an estate at Lebedin in Kharkov. In idyllic surroundings, fired by the success of *Aleko* and attention from his host's wife, Rachmaninoff composed easily. Three songs were completed and, together with three written earlier, were published by Gutheil as Opus 4. "Sing not to me, beautiful maiden" to a poem by Pushkin was dedicated to Natalia Satin, and became one of his more popular songs. At this time he also composed "The Harvest of Sorrow", also known in English as "O Thou my field", to a poem by Count Tolstoy, and "How Long, My Friend", a setting of a poem by Count Golenischev-Kuzutzov, which was dedicated to the poet's wife. A new work for two pianos followed swiftly: the *Fantasie-Tableaux* (also known as the Suite No 1) in four parts (or movements) — *Barcarolle*, *A Night for Love*, *Tears* and *Russian Easter*. Another work, for violin and piano, also appeared: *Two Pieces*, Opus 6, dedicated to Julius Conus[1], which are a *Romance* in D minor and a *Hungarian Dance*, similar to Opus 2 (the cello pieces for Brandukov). A liturgical work, for unaccompanied choir, "O Mother of God, vigilantly praying" was also written, and first performed in Moscow the following December 12th/25th by the Synodical Choir.

The proofs for the Opus 3 set had been corrected and their publication, at the time of the *Aleko* première, was a further step forward. Although the complete set is rarely played together, analysis reveals a subtle thematic unity. The most notable feature of the world-famous *Prelude* is its descending motif, and this is clearly echoed in the opening *Elégie* (one says echoed, as the *Prelude* was composed first). The faster chromatic section of the *Prelude* is linked to the themes of the remaining pieces. The final piece, the *Sérénade*, is distinctly European, having a gypsy-like Spanish flavour. In the two-piano *Fantasie-Tableaux* Rachmaninoff turned to Russian poetry for inspiration: apart from the opening *Barcarolle* (similar to the *Elégie* of Opus 3) the movements offer a succession of moods. Love, tears and, in the finale, joy, with a clattering evocation of a Russian Easter. The celebration of Easter has always meant a great deal to the Russian people. Rimsky-Korsakov's "Russian Easter Festival" Overture was the most famous musical celebration up to then, but Rachmaninoff's piece has more in common with Stravinsky's later *Petrushka* (1911) sharing the tumultuous activity which is a colourful feature of Stravinsky's opening *tableau*.

Encouraged by his growing reputation, Rachmaninoff tackled an orchestral work. His purely orchestral pieces until then had all been unsatisfactory, and none had been performed. He was attracted by a short story of Chekhov, *On the Road*, which in turn was prefaced by two lines from a poem by Lermontov, called *The Rock*. *The Rock* or, as it is sometimes known, *The Crag*, became the title of Rachmaninoff's piece, but he stated that the true source was the Chekhov story when he presented the author with a copy of the full score. He wrote on Chekhov's copy: "To dear and highly respected Anton Pavlovich Chekhov, author of the story *On the Road*, the plot of which . . . served as the programme for this work." It is a symphonic poem, owing a little to Liszt's *Les Préludes*: for those wishing to chart Rachmaninoff's progress as an orchestral composer it is significant, but only because compared to *Prince Rostislav* it has the virtue of relative brevity and concision. Both

Nikolai Andreyevitch Rimsky-Korsakov, 1844-1908.

[1] Whose brother, Lev Conus, was a composition finalist along with Rachmaninoff.

symphonic poems lack the lightness of texture which marked the 13-year-old's *Scherzo*, and the colour of the orchestral dances from *Aleko*.

As Rachmaninoff later recalled to Victor Babin, he had achieved much during the summer. He returned to Moscow with his growing portfolio, with still more ideas for composition. He took rooms, curiously enough in an apartment block called *America,* and by October had completed another group of songs, the six which comprise his Opus 8. The texts of three of these songs stem from Heine, and the Russian translation was by Plescheyev who, by a melancholy coincidence, had just died. Two of the others, also translated by the late poet, were of Ukranian origin. They form a fine set, including an absolute pearl "The Dream" (No 5) which was dedicated to Natalia Skalon, and from Goethe, "A Prayer" (No 6), dedicated to Maria Deisha-Sionitskaya the soprano who created the role of Zemfira in *Aleko*. The second song was dedicated to Slonov, but before they could be completed tragedy struck.

On September 30th/October 13th Nikolai Zverev died aged sixty-one. Many musicians, including Tchaikovsky, attended the funeral and Rachmaninoff met the older composer then at Taneyev's flat and showed him the *Fantasie-Tableaux*, obtaining permission to dedicate the work to him. The *Undine* business was finally settled: the libretto from Modest Tchaikovsky proved as unsatisfactory for Rachmaninoff as it had been for the librettist's brother, and a few days after Zverev's funeral he wrote to Modest shelving the project. The subject never arose again.

The success of *Aleko* led to an invitation for Rachmaninoff to conduct the opera himself in Kiev in October. He missed hearing Tchaikovsky conduct the first performance of his new *Pathétique* Symphony in St Petersburg on October 16th/29th, for on that day Rachmaninoff caught the train for Kiev. He directed the first two performances (his debût as an operatic conductor) and returned to Moscow to prepare for the imminent first performance of the *Fantasie-Tableaux* at the end of November. It was as well he was unable to travel to the capital for a cholera epidemic had broken out and Tchaikovsky, during lunch a few days after the première of the *Pathétique*, had incomprehensibly drunk some unboiled water. It was contaminated, and after a short illness he died on October 25th/November 7th.

Rachmaninoff was as deeply shocked and distressed at this news as was the whole musical world. The evening of Tchaikovsky's death he began a second *Trio Elégiaque* to the memory of the master. Work on the new trio was interrupted for the first performance of the *Fantasie-Tableaux*, whose dedication to Tchaikovsky assumed poignant significance, on November 30th/December 13th when Rachmaninoff was partnered by Pavel Pabst. A fortnight earlier in St Petersburg, at the Tchaikovsky memorial concert, the *Pathétique* received its second performance: the effect on the audience of the finale, the tragic *Adagio lamentoso*, can well be imagined. Rachmaninoff's own memorial to Tchaikovsky, the *Trio,*

Johann Wolfgang von Goethe (1749-1832)

Peter Jurgenson (1836-1904)

was finished on December 15th/28th three days after the choral anthem composed during the summer was premièred.

The year which began so promisingly ended with tragic blackness, but there were encouraging signs. The publication of the Opus 3 pieces was a commercial success and Alexander Siloti, on a visit to England in November, played the *Prelude* in C-sharp minor at St James's Hall in London. The resilience which Rachmaninoff had shown earlier enabled him to recover from the double-blow of the deaths of Zverev and Tchaikovsky, for in December he began a new set of piano pieces which he dedicated to Pabst as thanks for his collaboration in the *Fantasie-Tableaux* première. By the end of the year he completed three: a *Nocturne* in A minor, a *Waltz* in A major, and a *Barcarolle* in G minor. He probably also wrote the *Romance* for piano duet, and three further songs ("Song of the Disillusioned", "The Flower had faded", and "Do you Remember the Evening?") at this time, but the songs were never incorporated into a group.

The success of Gutheil's publications aroused the interest of rival companies. Jurgenson, who, with Tchaikovsky's death, lost his most important composer, turned to the young man who was rapidly making a name for himself. Although Gutheil had given Rachmaninoff a good start, he was unwilling to publish all his orchestral music, doubtless dissuaded by the greater cost compared to solo piano music which it entailed. When Jurgenson offered to publish the score of *The Rock*, Rachmaninoff felt no qualms in accepting. It also gave him the opportunity of associating with the publisher who had done much to help Tchaikovsky. In addition, Safonoff agreed to perform *The Rock* at a concert of the Russian Musical Society, by a happy coincidence on Rachmaninoff's twenty-first birthday.

First, there was an important all-Rachmaninoff concert at the end of January. At the beginning of the new year he composed four piano pieces, complementing those written in December, to form the seven *Morceaux de Salon* Opus 10 (the *Trio* was his Opus 9). Rachmaninoff played the *Morceaux* complete at the concert on January 31st/February 13th which also included, more importantly, the first performance of the second *Trio Elégiaque* by Rachmaninoff and Julius Conus (the dedicatee of Opus 6) and the faithful Brandukov. Apart from these two works, the concert also included Opus 2, Opus 6, some songs and Rachmaninoff playing the complete Opus 3 pieces.

It is difficult not to be deeply impressed by the second *Trio*: it is true the piano part is florid and of enormous difficulty (at one point, towards the end of the long first movement, it erupts into a quasi-cadenza), and the finale is possibly too short to balance the large dimensions of the first two movements — but what passion, what genuine depth of feeling, is contained in this work! Rachmaninoff's Opus 9 is a worthy memorial to Tchaikovsky.

In America, which Tchaikovsky visited three years before, his death was keenly felt, and the New York Symphony Orchestra lost no time in mounting a performance of the last symphony. On March 17th, Walter Damrosch conducted its U.S. première in Carnegie Hall. A fortnight later Rachmaninoff celebrated his twenty-first birthday, and attended the première that evening of *The Rock* in Moscow under Safonoff.

Rachmaninoff had by now taken a position as music-teacher at a ladies' Academy, where he remained for several years. He needed the income for his correspondence discloses he had little money. To augment his income he quickly wrote a set of piano-duets in a popular style which, although slight and of no great interest, form an attractive suite of delicate charm which might be enhanced by skilful orchestration. These six pieces reflect the salon-type music which was fashionable at the time. Rachmaninoff was not the only young serious composer to earn a living in this way: in Finland (then still part of the Russian Empire) Sibelius did the same thing. It is curious that Rachmaninoff did not teach at the Conservatory. As a Great Gold Medallist he was eminently qualified. Perhaps Sergei thought the demands as a professor would leave him little opportunity to compose. The ladies' Academy offered him greater freedom in that respect.

He must eagerly have looked forward to the summer, for it again meant an idyllic interlude at Ivanovka with his cousins and the opportunity to compose at will. He took up the score of the Gypsy Fantasia, which he had begun two summers previously but had been unable to work on since the flood of music in other forms the year before. The première of *The Rock* probably spurred him on and the score, his Opus 12, was completed at Ivanovka. He read the proofs of Jurgenson's score of *The Rock* at Kostroma where he had gone to give lessons, and even sketched ideas for a new symphonic poem based on Byron's *Don Juan* in Count Tolstoy's translation. A "Chorus of Spirits" survives, but another song was written at Ivanovka which he dedicated to Natalia Skalon, "I Wait for Thee": this was carefully put on one side to await further songs for publication as a group.

In New York the amazing Thomas Alva Edison demonstrated on April 14th his Kinetoscope, a forerunner of the modern cinema, in public at 1155 Broadway. Edison's earlier invention, the phonograph, was developed further by Emile Berliner who demonstrated a horizontal disc, maintaining it afforded better sound reproduction, but it was not until a further three years before it became satisfactory.

On his return to Moscow Rachmaninoff was nagged by several doubts. He finished the score of the Gypsy Fantasia calling it *Caprice Bohémien (Capriccio on Gypsy Themes)*, and dedicated it to Peter Lodischensky, whose wife Anna was of gypsy extraction. Zverev, the Tchaikovskys, the Rubinstein brothers and many of the intelligentsia in Russia were fascinated by gypsy life. Clubs, restaurants and bars in the cities frequently engaged gypsy singers and dancers and, in the decades towards the end of the nineteenth century, gypsy folk-song and folk-life became a very popular form of escapism, a throw-back to a less regimented society than was both evolving and being imposed within Russia. Rachmaninoff was introduced to gypsy music by Zverev and came to love it, and traces of gypsy-like influences can be found in Rachmaninoff's work from time to time. Apart from large works like *Aleko* (with its story of gypsy life) and the *Caprice Bohémien,* smaller works show this influence, and Anna Lodischensky exerted a fascination for Rachmaninoff. He had become enamoured of her, and dedicated to her the first of the Opus 4 songs ("Oh No, I beg You, Forsake Me Not"): but a much bigger work was looming in his mind.

His thoughts again turned to composition: what was required was an important work. His musical sensibility had been groping towards this objective for some time. The projected symphonic poem of the previous summer bears that out, and in January 1895 he settled down to work on his first 'real' symphony, Opus 13.

Once again D minor was the key, and it is interesting to see how often this key occurred in his work. His first orchestral work, the *Scherzo,* is in D minor, and so is the earlier one-movement Symphony. *Prince Rostislav* is also in D minor, and *Aleko* is based on this key as well. D minor is the tonality of many of Rachmaninoff's songs and piano pieces, and the second *Trio Elégiaque* is also in D minor. Whatever the fascination this particular tonality had for Rachmaninoff, it was certainly strong, so it was almost inevitable that the First Symphony should be set in that key. In another sense, because of the symphony's tremendous artistic advance, it was possibly the work towards which he had subconsciously been striving for several years.

Jean Sibelius, 1865-1957.

Once he began the Symphony in January it consumed him. Working with that growing certainty which comes to artists when they know they are creating something worthwhile, with ever-increasing confidence he finished the work, easily his greatest composition up to that time, on August 30th/September 12th at Ivanovka. The score bore the somewhat cryptic dedication to "A.L." (Anna Lodischensky).

Apart from his teaching at the ladies' Academy, Rachmaninoff received little income whilst writing the Symphony, so to earn more money he undertook a three-month concert tour once the Symphony was finished with the Italian violinist Teresina Tua. Rachmaninoff's old friend Sakhnovsky, who tended him while he was ill during his last year at the Conservatory, and who was now well-connected in Moscow musical circles, asked the publisher and impressario Belaieff if he could do something for the young composer. Sergei had good friends: Taneyev and Glazunov also approached Belaieff with the same idea, and the St Petersburg musician agreed to programme *The Rock* for performance early in 1896.

Belaieff was then fifty-nine and, being the son of a wealthy timber-merchant and a great music-lover, had formed a successful music publishing house in 1885 in Leipzig, as Germany was covered by international copyright (Russia at that time was not). In

35

the same year he sponsored a series of Russian Symphony Concerts in St Petersburg. He also helped Rachmaninoff in another way: as Glazunov's publisher, he issued piano-duet editions of his orchestral works, and Belaieff asked Sergei to prepare a duet version of Glazunov's new Sixth Symphony which he could only accommodate after the tour with Teresina Tua.

No sooner had they given the first concert of the tour in Lodz than Rachmaninoff had second thoughts as to the wisdom of proceeding. The tour opened on November 7th/20th, but two days later Rachmaninoff wrote to Slonov saying although the concert had been a popular success, it had not been an artistic one. Apparently the Contessa Teresina Tua-Franchi-Verney della Valetta (the violinist's full name) was more pleasing to look at than to hear, and she was also extremely mean. It was not long before the tour brought them to Moscow where on November 22nd/December 5th Rachmaninoff conducted the first performance of the *Caprice Bohémien*. Some commentators feel this work lacks any advance over *The Rock,* but it is certainly far less pretentious than the earlier symphonic poem. A typical piece of the Russian nationalist school, short and rhapsodic, it displays characteristics of the later Rachmaninoff. It was quite clearly modelled on the Caprices of both Rimsky-Korsakov and Tchaikovsky (Spanish and Italian respectively), and those works are not examples of either composers' art at its finest. Rachmaninoff was grateful for the inclusion of Moscow in the tour itinerary because he was able to conduct the *Caprice* and also resign from the rest of the tour, claiming he had not been paid for the concerts he had given.

This enabled him to concentrate on other projects: the transcription of Glazunov's Sixth Symphony, and a set of six choruses for women's (or children's) voices and piano — a direct result of his teaching post at the ladies' Academy — published as Opus 15, as well as another set of songs, the twelve which comprise Opus 14 (the first, "I Wait For Thee", dates from 1894). The remainder were all written in 1896, two of which, "The Little Island" and "Spring Waters", are among the cream of his songs. "Spring Waters" is also notable for its extremely difficult piano part (similar to many songs from the set), but that may be due to the fact that the song is dedicated to his first piano teacher, Anna Ornatskaya.

In January 1896, before all these pieces were written, Rachmaninoff again travelled to St Petersburg where he heard Glazunov's performance of *The Rock* on January 20th/February 2nd at the Belaieff Russian Symphony Concert. Belaieff agreed to include the new Symphony the following season also under Glazunov, so the reception was obviously cordial. Rachmaninoff was naturally delighted at the prospect.

The year was spent working intermittently: the prospect of the symphony's performance continually distracted him, and he probably composed at this time two movements for string quartet, in G minor and C minor. They were first performed posthumously

Alexander Konstantinovitch Glazunov, 1865-1936.

The Moscow Conservatory

Cesar Cui (1835-1918)

in Moscow in October 1945 by the Beethoven Quartet, in the same concert at which the movements from 1889 were also heard for the first time. Rachmaninoff probably composed his contribution to a series of *Four Improvisations* for solo piano at this time, the other three being by Arensky, Glazunov and Taneyev. Towards the end of the year, Rachmaninoff began serious composition again: six *Moments Musicaux* for solo piano were written between October and December. These were something else: the mature Rachmaninoff, already present in the Symphony, was here revealed for the first time in his solo piano music. These *Moments Musicaux* Opus 16, dedicated to Alexander Zatayevitch, mark a turning-point in his career as a composer, being by far his greatest work for solo piano up to then.

Glazunov confirmed the date for the first performance of the Symphony as March 15th/28th in the capital. Rachmaninoff travelled to St Petersburg for the rehearsals, which did not go well. Compared with *The Rock*, the Symphony is hardly recognisable as being by the same composer. It is a tricky score for both conductor and orchestra, and its length (45 minutes) was probably rather more than Glazunov had expected. Its language was also modern and new — in contrast with Glazunov's own Sixth Symphony, written (apart from the finale) in a conservative style. The scherzo in Rachmaninoff's Symphony doubtless gave trouble, for a cut of thirty-six bars was marked on the orchestral parts — by no means the last time Rachmaninoff agreed to cuts in his works. More changes, especially in the orchestration, were made by Glazunov. The actual text of the work — apart from the cut — was unchanged, but the character of many passages was altered by Glazunov's re-casting.

Whatever the reasons, the première of the Symphony was catastrophic. As the last bars were played Rachmaninoff fled from the hall and paced aimlessly up and down the streets, beside himself with a mixture of fury and despair at the ruinous performance of the work which he had been eagerly awaiting for almost two years. The press had a field day — bad premières are always the composer's fault in most critics eyes. The old feud between the cities sprang up again: Cesar Cui, then 62, gave the worst notice of Rachmaninoff's life and others were not much better.

For Sergei it was a dreadful experience: he was actually indifferent to the failure of the work, but what hurt him was the knowledge that he had written his greatest work and created a masterly composition, only to hear it murdered by a ham-fisted conductor. The cryptic dedication to the woman to whom he had formed an attachment meant the Symphony was a token of things other than musical, for the original score carried a quotation from Romans XII, v.19: "Vengeance is mine; I will repay, saith the Lord", which also appears in Leo Tolstoy's *Anna Karenina*. Tolstoy's novel concerns a young woman of society who made a loveless marriage with a civil servant older than herself. She falls in love with a young army officer and her love for him finally ends in her suicide. If Rachmaninoff's attachment to Anna Lodischensky had become as deep as some believed, then the connection between the two Annas is clear and the Biblical quotation explained. In addition there is a musical link between the Symphony and 'her' song, published as Opus 4 No 1: the main musical idea for the Symphony is derived from the song's piano accompaniment. The Symphony meant more to Rachmaninoff than many supposed.

In a letter to Zatayevitch, two months later, Rachmaninoff's reactions to the première are remarkably level-headed, laying the blame quite squarely on Glazunov. He knew the Symphony possessed unique qualities, which have still not been fully appreciated today, even by students of the composer. Initially Rachmaninoff had no intention of destroying the work but felt some editing might be necessary. Indeed, the following year he made a piano-duet version which Gutheil published, but the Symphony was never performed again during the composer's lifetime. The original score was either lost or destroyed and it was not

Anna Karenina watches as Count Vronsky falls within sight of the winning post *(Painting by A.V. Vanezian)*.

until after Rachmaninoff's death that the original parts came to light and the score was reconstructed, using the published piano-duet version as a guide. The second performance took place in Moscow in 1945, and the first American performance on March 19th 1948, by the Philadelphia Orchestra under Eugene Ormandy. They naturally used the edition then recently published in the U.S.S.R., but the parts on which the score was based were those altered by Glazunov. In 1977 the State Publishing House in Moscow issued a new critical edition of the Symphony, reverting to the parts as first copied before Glazunov changed them. This is the most authentic score in existence, and all subsequent performances should be given from it, and not from the now discredited Glazunov edition. It is only since World War II therefore that Rachmaninoff's First Symphony has come to be known at all, and its originality and quality are still not generally recognised. Possibly the best assessment of this work is that by Robert Simpson:

. . . It is a powerful work in its own right, stemming from Tchaikovsky and Borodin, but convinced, individual, finely constructed, and achieving a genuinely tragic and heroic expression . . . as an artistic whole, created naturally and without strain it leaves little to be desired . . . And at no time is it ever less than intensely personal, strongly compelling. All four movements are genuinely thematically integrated . . .

This First Symphony is a real masterpiece: the tiny motto theme with which it opens begins, in altered form, each of the four movements, and a second motto theme, heard shortly after, is threaded through the score with a subtlety and care that bears the closest analysis. In the coda of the finale, its resemblance to the plainchant *Dies Irae* theme is revealed — surely a reference to the fate of *Anna Karenina* — and, in view of Rachmaninoff's later use of the plainchant theme, highly significant. The orchestration, especially in the scherzo, is breathtakingly deft and assured. There is little doubt that this impressive work should be performed as frequently as Rachmaninoff's later symphonies.

5   New Directions

In spite of the public humiliation of the première of the Symphony, the letter to Zatayevitch shows the composer's calm and confident state of mind. Three weeks after the scandal, while visiting his grandparents in Novgorod, he sketched ideas for a new Symphony but they came to nothing. The letter, however, does not tell the full story. Rachmaninoff was affected by the failure of the Symphony and, on his return to Moscow, he gave up his rooms in the *America* apartment-house and spent the summer with the Skalons on their estate. But this summer was one without composition. That he knew the originality and worth of his Symphony is beyond dispute: his musical sensibility must have told him that to pursue the line of the work would have taken him into areas fraught with artistic and commercial disaster. This possibly led him to abandon the sketches for the new Symphony but, such was his all-round musical ability (he had already conducted in the concert-hall and the opera house), he might have felt his future (financially, at any rate) lay in a conducting career. If Glazunov could get away with it, surely he could do much better? As if to answer these imaginings, Rachmaninoff received a marvellous offer.

A wealthy Moscow businessman who had made a fortune from the railways founded the Moscow Private Russian Opera Company in 1885, and for the 1897-98 season invited Rachmaninoff to become deputy conductor. The man was Savva Mamontov, who possessed as shrewd a judgement for music as he had shown in his business dealings for he engaged many gifted artists. Among them at that time was the young bass Feodor Chaliapin, who was Rachmaninoff's exact contemporary, being less than two months older than Sergei.

Rachmaninoff accepted Mamontov's offer eagerly, but he had little inkling of the talent or methods of the musical director, an Italian called Esposito who, on hearing the news of Rachmaninoff's appointment, began to fear for his own. He suggested Rachmaninoff conduct Glinka's *A Life for the Tsar* but he only allowed one rehearsal, with the result that the performance was in danger: to save the situation, Esposito 'agreed' to conduct. Rachmaninoff, however, had his superb training and memory to fall back on: he grasped the essential features of his task very quickly, and for his debût on October 12th/25th conducted Saint-Saëns's *Samson et Dalila*, forming a close friendship with Chaliapin, which lasted until Chaliapin's death. He then conducted Dargomïjsky's *Rusalka* with Chaliapin, and was highly praised by the press. Other operas conducted by Rachmaninoff during this season, which was proving successful, were Bizet's *Carmen*, Gluck's *Orphée* and, early in 1898, Rimsky-Korsakov's *May Night*, again with Chaliapin. This suffered somewhat as the theatre the company had been using burned down and the new home was less congenial, making adjustment difficult.

However, Rachmaninoff was clearly a competent operatic conductor and he liked the job enormously. It was a pity that events happening in America had not occurred a little earlier. In February 1897 Fred Gaisberg established the world's first gramophone recording studio, over a shoe shop on 12th street in Philadelphia. In view of what was soon to happen, it would have been possible for recordings to have been made of extracts from these performances with Rachmaninoff conducting.

Mamontov was pleased with his young conductor and retained him for the following season. During the summer, Rachmaninoff and Chaliapin stayed with other members of the Opera at Putyantino, in Yaroslav, which belonged to a friend of Mamontov. They spent many hours studying Mussorgsky's *Boris Godunov*, which was scheduled for the following season. Rachmaninoff had to decline an invitation from Alexander Goldenweiser for a new Piano Concerto, owing to pressure of work and because ideas were not flowing as freely as they had a year or two before. The inspiration now was for stage works: he again approached Modest Tchaikovsky for a libretto, on Shakespeare's Richard II, possibly with Chaliapin in mind. Modest declined, but suggested *Francesca da Rimini* instead: this was a novel idea for Rachmaninoff and one which greatly appealed to him. But he had to shelve his plans as preparations for the new season, a short illness, a brief concert tour, as well as the duet version of the Symphony, all left him no time for composition.

He was pleased to learn of Alexander Siloti's successful European tour during which Rachmaninoff's *Prelude* in C-sharp minor was received with the greatest possible enthusiasm, particularly in England, where, on February 22nd in the small Queen's Hall, his *Trio Elégiaque* No 2 was played for the first time, at a Walenn Chamber Concert, by the brothers Gerald and Herbert Walenn, with Herbert Parsons, piano.

Meanwhile, the repressive regime of Alexander III, who had died in 1894, was tempered by his far less despotic son, Nicholas II, and by the fiscal policies of the remarkable Minister of Finance, Sergei Witte, who did much to create a thriving economic climate. However, nothing could disguise the iron grip of the Tsar. In the 1890s many Russians emigrated like Morris Gershovitz, the son of the St Petersburg gunsmith. Gershovitz met Rose Bruskin in St

Petersburg and when her family emigrated to the United States he followed them. The immigration authorities entered his name as 'Gershvine': shortly after his arrival, he married Rose. Their first son Ira was born on December 6th 1896, and a second son Jacob followed on September 26th 1898. To the baby's brother, Ira, the boy was always known as 'George'.

Siloti's success in England resulted in Rachmaninoff being invited by the Royal Philharmonic Society of London to appear in the Queen's Hall to play and conduct his own music. It was a great honour which he accepted, but it had to wait until the second season at the opera was finished. Once it was over he travelled to London, making the 1,937-mile journey in two-and-a-half days, changing trains at Warsaw owing to the difference in track widths.

Rachmaninoff managed to compose two piano pieces before he left for London early in 1899: a *Morceau de Fantasie* in G minor on January 11th/24th, and a *Fughetta* in F major on February 4th/17th, just three weeks before Gustav Mahler conducted the first complete performance of Bruckner's Sixth Symphony in Vienna, and a month before Richard Strauss conducted the première of *Ein Heldenleben* in Frankfurt on March 3rd — a work dedicated to Willem Mengelberg, the conductor of the Concertgebouw Orchestra of Amsterdam. Rachmaninoff appeared at the Queen's Hall London on April 19th playing the by-now famous *Prelude,* and the *Elégie* from the same set. He conducted an aria from Borodin's *Prince Igor* and *The Rock.* The reviews were somewhat non-committal, but so far as one can judge the concert was a success. Rachmaninoff was invited to return the following year to play his Concerto. Although Rachmaninoff accepted he told the Royal Philharmonic Society that he would compose a new Concerto for the occasion. Evidently he was dissatisfied with the F-sharp minor. Had he stayed longer in London he would have been able to attend the première of Edward Elgar's *"Enigma" Variations* in St James's Hall, exactly two months to the day after his own debût, conducted by Hans Richter. However, his return to Russia was swift for he had to prepare for a concert performance of *Aleko,* as part of the Pushkin centenary celebrations. Rachmaninoff was doubly excited by the prospect of these celebrations for it meant he would have the chance to conduct his work again, and Chaliapin would be making his debût in the title role. Chaliapin was also looking forward to the concert. Later in life Chaliapin always maintained Rachmaninoff was his ideal conductor. As Ivor Newton, the great piano accompanist, wrote:

. . . He would say, 'When Rachmaninoff conducted for me, or accompanied me at the piano, we sang as one man.'

At the performance, Chaliapin was inspired: Rachmaninoff recalled how

. . . he sobbed at the end of the opera. Only a great actor, or a man who had experienced such sorrow as *Aleko* had can sob like that.

42

Feodor Chaliapin, the great
Russian bass, in the title
rôle of *Boris Godunov*.

In spite of his success at the People's Opera Rachmaninoff resigned at the end of the second season, and he had not been excited by his London performance as he should have been. The performance of *Aleko*, however memorable artistically it had been, did not seem to fire his enthusiasm greatly. For the first time in his life, but certainly not the last, Rachmaninoff felt his career as a composer was suffering as a result of the demands of his other careers as pianist and conductor. But the freedom which his resignation gave him was not matched by a flood of inspiration: at a time when he should have been feeling on top of the world, Rachmaninoff was going through a difficult phase. It is frequently supposed that the failure of the Symphony brought on a period of depression, but Rachmaninoff's hectic activity during the succeeding eighteen months clearly shows he had little time for composition, even if he had had the inclination. Now the opportunity was there (and the promise for a new Concerto for London), but he was not able to seize it. Possibly the ending of his relationship with Anna Lodischensky contributed to this feeling of lassitude, which became so marked that his family and friends became concerned. Rachmaninoff was not ill physically or even mentally — he was simply unable to work.

His cousin's family, the Satins, came to his help. They mentioned Rachmaninoff's condition to a friend, Princess Alexandra Leivin (whose sister was Director of the Smolnyi Institute in St Petersburg) who knew Leo Tolstoy. As Rachmaninoff deeply admired Tolstoy, the Princess arranged for Sergei to meet the great man, who possessed a considerable knowledge of music, in the hope that the experience would inspire him. She primed Tolstoy as to Rachmaninoff's condition, but the first meeting on February 1st/14th was hopeless. Rachmaninoff later recalled:

. . . He saw how nervous I was. And then, at table, he said to me, 'You must work. Do you think that I am pleased with myself? Work. I must work every day', and similar sterotyped phrases.

A second visit was arranged, this time with Chaliapin, who recalled:

. . . For the first time in my life I was to see Tolstoy face to face, a man whose thoughts and words had already touched the world. Hitherto I had only seen him in photographs, and now here he was in person, standing near the chess table, talking to Alexander Goldenweiser. My first surprise was to realise that he was shorter than medium height. In the photographs he had seemed so tall . . . How simply and charmingly he took my hand, how ordinary the questions he asked me. How long had I been in the theatre? How boyish I looked. Rachmaninoff was a little braver than I, and yet he too was excited, and his hands were quite cold. He whispered in my ear, 'If they ask me to play I don't honestly know if I'll be able to. My hands are like ice'. And Tolstoy did ask him to play. I can't recall what he played, I only know of my own worrying thought. 'Suppose he asks me to sing'. My heart went further into my boots, when Tolstoy looked Rachmaninoff straight in the eye and asked, 'Tell me, does anyone want this type of music?'

43

For someone in Rachmaninoff's state of mind and in the company of a friend, the question could not have been more demoralising. This second attempt to get Sergei working again proved equally disastrous. The pieces he had written since leaving the People's Opera, including an arrangement of two folk songs, one Russian and the other Ukranian, for chorus, were all trifles. Only one, the folk-song "Shoes", survives. These were composed towards the end of 1899 before Tolstoy's visits. At that time, on November 18th in Buda-Pest, Eugene Ormandy was born.

Something other than temporary loss of inspiration was troubling Rachmaninoff and causing concern to his relatives and friends. It was clear to the Satin family that medical help should be sought and he himself also felt the need for assistance. The spread of psychiatry in Europe had been rapid, and in 1900 Sigmund Freud was to publish his most important work, *Traumdeutung* (The Interpretation of Dreams). Rachmaninoff agreed to visit Dr Nikolai Dahl, who practiced in Moscow specialising in neurology and hypnosis. Dr Dahl was also a keen amateur musician, so this connection between the two men was undoubtedly helpful. He also knew of Rachmaninoff's work and so had a point of immediate contact with his patient which another doctor might have spent weeks trying to establish.

For several months Rachmaninoff visited Dr Dahl. Later he recalled that he was subjected to simple but effective treatment, including a form of hypnosis. He was almost invariably half-asleep while Dr Dahl repeated over and over the suggestive phrases "You will begin to write your Concerto . . . you will work with great facility . . . the Concerto will be of excellent quality . . ." In effect Dr Dahl was stating, with infinitely more subtlety and understanding and with a more sympathetic emphasis, the same suggestion given as advice by Leo Tolstoy: "You must work".

It is also clear from Rachmaninoff's recollections of his treatment that he was concerned over his promise to the Royal Philharmonic Society for a new Concerto, for the idea for the work can hardly have come from Dr Dahl himself. Rachmaninoff was obviously worried about the lack of ideas for the work and his inability to write it which would mean breaking his promise to the Society.

After the treatment was over Rachmaninoff stayed with Chaliapin in the southern Crimea where the climate was noted for its therapeutic qualities. While there, Chaliapin received a telegram from the La Scala opera in Milan inviting him to sing the title role in Boito's *Mefistofele*. At first he treated it as a joke, but his wife (who was Italian and had been a ballerina in Mamontov's company) urged him to take it seriously. She persuaded him to answer, requesting that the message be repeated. The reply convinced him it was genuine but, as he knew no Italian and had little time to prepare the part, he sent off a message of acceptance, demanding exorbitant terms, secretly hoping the opera house would refuse. To his astonished delight his demands were met and so the Chaliapins, accompanied by Rachmaninoff, travelled to Varazze, a little resort

Rachmaninoff and
Chaliapin, c.1898.

Detail from a portrait by Ivan Kramskoi of the celebrated Russian writer Leo Tolstoy.

on the way to San Remo. They stayed at a small villa, lived frugally (to enable Chaliapin to get his voice in trim and for financial reasons), and found the Italians friendly and hospitable. The local shopkeepers, when they discovered their visitors were preparing for a performance at La Scala, did everything to help. In this relaxed and congenial atmosphere, with all the new images and interests the first visit to a foreign country always brings, Rachmaninoff found his inspiration returning. He began several works and completed a setting, appropriately enough, of Count Tolstoy's "Panteley the Healer" (*Panteley-tselitel*). The study of opera also rekindled his plans for *Francesca da Rimini*, and he composed the love-duet. His letters suggest it was some time before he settled down to composition, but it was a good sign to his friends in Russia to read in his correspondence that noise prevented him writing his music.

The two main works which he sketched out in Italy were completed on his return to Russia: the first was a Second Suite for two pianos, Opus 17, which he began in December 1900, and — much more importantly — the new Concerto.

Rachmaninoff's illness and his travels with Chaliapin meant that Fred Gaisberg, the young American recording pioneer (the results of whose Philadelphia studio were already highly significant), was unable to get either Chaliapin or Rachmaninoff to record for him

45

when he visited St Petersburg in March and April. Gaisberg visited the city following the recommendations of two early gramophone dealers there, but on arrival it was clear to him the agents had done nothing to line up possible recording artists, nor were they as well-connected as his employers had been led to believe. The recording team made some records of popular artists, but Chaliapin, who had just scored a great success in the capital in Glinka's *A Life for the Tsar*, refused Gaisberg's advances. Gaisberg recorded other singers from the Opera, and Taneyev was persuaded to record a short piano piece of his own. On his return from Russia Gaisberg would have been fascinated to learn of the plans afoot in Philadelphia to found a new symphony orchestra. This finally materialised on November 16th, when the Philadelphia Orchestra gave its first concert in the Academy of Music (itself constructed many years earlier from designs based on the interior of La Scala). The conductor was Fritz Scheel, and the soloist, in Tchaikovsky's Piano Concerto in B-flat minor, was Ossip Gabrilowitsch. The programme also included Beethoven's Fifth Symphony and an overture by Karl Goldmark, "In Spring".

In England Sergei's fame was growing: on October 4th, 1900, his First Piano Concerto had its British première with Evelyn Stuart, and the Queen's Hall Orchestra conducted by Henry J. Wood. For Wood, it was one of his first performances of Rachmaninoff's music, with which he had a special empathy, encouraged by the Russian Princess Olga Ouroussoff whom he had recently married.

Rachmaninoff's pleasure at the news of the Concerto was muted as he now thought it an unrepresentative work. This October, fired with ideas for the new Concerto which came to him in Italy, he worked at his old speed and the work was soon drafted. Or rather the last two movements were: the first movement followed later, and it was probably Siloti's enthusiasm for the two completed movements on hearing Sergei play them through, that led to them being performed for the first time, in Moscow, on December 2nd/15th. This took place in the Hall of the Nobility, which stood in the corner of *Okhotni Ryad* Square, at that time a famous stall-market for vegetables, poultry and eggs. Sergei agreed to the work being played incomplete, for the first movement was not ready: Siloti was to conduct. As the time of the concert approached, Sergei caught a heavy cold, which threatened complications. As the Concerto was unfinished, Rachmaninoff possibly altered the opening of the slow movement. The Concerto is in C minor, but the slow movement is in E, so to make a suitable beginning, he could have altered the opening bars later, as they begin in the home key (C minor), and gently modulate to E. For some listeners, especially die-hard conservatives, the shock of hearing a work begin in a key other than the stated one would have been too much.

Sergei overcame the cold and the performance was tremendously successful. Friends and relatives including Princess Leivin and the Satin family were in the audience to see his triumph. In the slow movement, Sergei paid a musical compliment to another family

46

Manuscript of the first page of the First Piano Concerto

First page of an unpublished piano piece, 1917

who had helped him so much, the Skalons, by basing the piano's gently-flowing cross-rhythm on the *Romance* he had written for the three sisters nine years before. And to Dr Dahl, the catalyst of the work, he paid a more subtle tribute: a curious characteristic of the concerto's orchestration is the frequent use Rachmaninoff makes of the viola section — especially in the finale. As Dr Dahl was an accomplished viola-player he must have smiled to himself as he heard his favourite instrument being featured in the score.

The success of the performance spurred Rachmaninoff to finish the work on April 21st/May 4th 1901. In April he also completed the Second Suite for two pianos, like the First (the *Fantasie-Tableaux*), in four movements but without an explicit literary source. During the composition of the new Suite, Rachmaninoff showed it to Goldenweiser, the pianist and disciple of Tolstoy. As Goldenweiser was present at the visit of Rachmaninoff and Chaliapin to Tolstoy, and witnessed Rachmaninoff's condition, he must have been surprised at Sergei's new-found confidence. When the Suite was finished, Rachmaninoff dedicated it to Goldenweiser, and he inscribed the Concerto to Dr Dahl. Apart from the Suite and the Concerto, another work was running through Rachmaninoff's mind. It was eight years since he had written chamber music, and he now planned a Sonata for Cello and Piano. During the summer, he wrote the Sonata, and the character of the piece shows the confidence and flood of creative energy which consumed him.

By the autumn of 1901 Rachmaninoff had three new works ready. All were scheduled for performance in Moscow by the end of that year, but the first was the most important: the première of the entire Second Concerto, Opus 18, with Rachmaninoff as soloist with the orchestra of the Moscow Philharmonic Society, again under his cousin Alexander Siloti. It took place on October 27th/November 9th and the reception accorded the complete work was greater than that which attended the incomplete performance the previous December. Rachmaninoff had already in the First Symphony proved he could construct big works with a subtlety and integration that was equalled by few contemporaries. In the Second Concerto he demonstrated this capacity once again in a work which genuinely moved the audience. The eight opening chords of the slow movement were metamorphosed into the famous inception of eight piano chords which begin the Concerto, quietly insistent and, with internal counterpoint, growing to the home key and the first theme. The score is full of superb touches, frequently overlooked by those who are carried away (or put off) by the top layer of its rich melodic substance. In a word the Concerto is inspired, but Rachmaninoff was too good a composer not to let the beautiful creation be based on less than solid foundations. Since that first performance the Concerto has become one of the most popular and frequently-played in the repertory but it is curious that, with two recordings by Rachmaninoff, the work is usually played a good deal slower than the composer played it, or marked it.

A few weeks later, Rachmaninoff and Siloti collaborated in

Rachmaninoff — an informal study dating from about 1900.

47

another première: the Second Suite, Opus 17. This, the first work completed after the return of his creative spark, shows his high flood of inspiration. The opening of the Second Suite in comparison with the First is confident and strong, full of nervous energy. The notes cascade with exhilarating speed, and this tingling sensation is carried over into the second movement, a scintillating *Waltz*. Even the *Romance* flows along and the final *Tarentella* is positively giddy. It is a dazzling work, easily superior to the First Suite. A deeper and more personal utterance is found in the Cello Sonata. Rachmaninoff and Siloti played the Suite on November 24th/December 7th with the dedicatee, Alexander Goldenweiser, in the audience. Eight days later Rachmaninoff and Brandukov premièred the Cello Sonata. Brandukov therefore took part in the first performances of all Rachmaninoff's chamber works in which a cello is called for. It may be that revisions were made after the première as the score is dated December 12th, ten days after the first performance.

The new century (the difference between the Julian and the Gregorian calendars increased to thirteen days on January 1st, 1901) also saw the ends and beginnings of new eras. In January Queen Victoria of Britain died and the Edwardian age ushered in by her 60-year-old son was vastly different. A few days later on January 27th Verdi died aged 87, having lived to see the success of his compatriot, Puccini, whose opera *Tosca* was premièred a year before. In America, the smouldering resentments of immigrant anarchists took tangible form when, on September 6th, President William McKinley, welcoming visitors to the Pan-American Exhibition in Buffalo, New York, was shot by Leon Czolgosz, a terrorist. He died eight days later and was succeeded as twenty-eighth President by Theodore Roosevelt. On November 16th in New York, the young Josef Hofmann (then 25), a colleague of Rachmaninoff, made his debût with the New York Philharmonic.

Fred Gaisberg journeyed to Philadelphia in 1901 (his success in the early years of the gramophone industry led to him being stationed in Europe, where he played a major role in founding and developing the Gramophone Company, whose trademark was "His Master's Voice"). On his arrival in Philadelphia he found that another early gramophone pioneer, Eldridge Johnson, had overcome serious technical and commercial difficuties and persuaded Emile Berliner to join forces with him. Johnson named the new company, following his success, the Victor company.

Rachmaninoff, apart from the success of his new works, had another reason to feel pleased. Since he arrived in Moscow at the age of 12 (he was now 29), his aunts and uncles had taken a kindly interest in his affairs and Rachmaninoff had been attracted by the pretty young girls who were his cousins. The affair with "A.L." was long over and Rachmaninoff startled his relatives by declaring, early in 1902, his intention of marrying his cousin Natalia Satin. Apart from being pleasantly surprised at his announcement there was concern, for Rachmaninoff and Natalia were first cousins, and

Josef Hofmann with the composer in the late 1890s.

48

This photograph of the composer at the age of 29 was taken by the father of Boris Pasternak, author of *Doctor Zhivago*.

marriage between first cousins was forbidden under the laws of the Russian Orthodox Church. Furthermore both parties had to be regular churchgoers, and Rachmaninoff's attendances had lapsed. Several weeks passed before the problems were resolved.

Natalia had also graduated as a pianist from the Moscow Conservatory and her innate musicianship was an additional bond between the couple. Their cousin, Alexander Siloti, who conducted the first performance of the Second Concerto, now gave the première in St Petersburg on March 15th/28th, playing the solo part with Arthur Nikisch conducting. It was a tremendous success in the capital, and Siloti and Nikisch repeated the Concerto in Leipzig with the Gewandhaus Orchestra, before Siloti brought the Concerto to England on tour.

Before then the busy Siloti conducted another Rachmaninoff première. Rachmaninoff was eager to compose something for Chaliapin and by February 1902 he completed his first choral work, the Cantata "Spring" (*Vesna*), Opus 20, for baritone solo, chorus and orchestra. It tells of a peasant couple, the wife's admission of infidelity so incensing her husband that he resolves to kill her. The first rays of the coming of Spring make him relent.

Rachmaninoff's reputation now ensured that each new work would be performed quickly, and Siloti was able to première "Spring" on March 11th/24th. This was too soon for Chaliapin (the work was not dedicated to him, but to Nikita Morozov, a fellow-competitor in setting *Aleko*), so the solo was sung by Alexei Smirnoff. "Spring" is a neglected masterpiece — an imaginative evocation of time and place, typically Russian. The quality of musical invention is very high and Rachmaninoff was clearly deeply moved by the final message of the poem, which may well have had personal significance for him:

Love while it is yet possible to love,
Bear while it is yet possible to bear,
Forgive while it is yet possible to forgive,
And God will be your judge.

"Spring" is a dramatic work, a precursor of Rachmaninoff's later operas, and Shostakovitch's "Execution of Stepan Razin", with which it could usefully be paired in concert.

Rachmaninoff's marriage plans needed settling. Another aunt, Anna Trubnikova, spoke to Father Amphitheatrov who was attached to the Archanglesky Cathedral. Whilst bribery possibly played a part in overcoming the problems, Rachmaninoff later spoke of Father Amphitheatrov with genuine affection, in terms which do not suggest this. Because of the military connections of the Rachmaninoff family, it was possible for the marriage to take place in a garrison chapel rather than a normal church. The advantage of this was that the military chaplains were responsible to the General Staff of the Army and not to the ecclesiastical authorities, with the result that the strict doctrine of the Orthodox

49

The composer with his wife Natalia.

Church was by-passed. Consequently, Sergei and Natalia were married in the chapel of the Tavrichensky Regiment in the suburbs of Moscow, on April 29th/May 12th 1902. Alexander Siloti and Anatole Brandukov were chief witnesses and best men. The following day, after a reception which included many members of the large family, the newly-weds left for an extended honeymoon abroad.

They visited Vienna and Venice and spent some time in Lucerne before returning home via Bayreuth, where they attended performances of *The Flying Dutchman,* the complete *Ring,* and *Parsifal,* and witnessed the Bayreuth debût of Emil Borgmann as Erik in Siegfried Wagner's second season as manager. While staying in Lucerne, Sergei completed eleven songs (inspired by marriage as Schumann had been) to add to 'Fate', the song he wrote previously for Chaliapin, and all twelve were published as Opus 21. These songs, apart from 'Fate', which recalls the opening motif of Beethoven's Fifth Symphony, are among the most intimate of Rachmaninoff's songs: the dedications to several of the couple's friends at this time of great personal happiness confirm this, but the piano part, more restrained and less florid than his previous set (Opus 14), underlines the poise which now entered his music. The third song, "Twilight" is dedicated to the designer of Mamontov's Opera Company; the sixth (a Fragment from Alfred de Musset) to Princess Lieven, and the twelfth to his mother-in-law Varvara. The fifth, 'Lilacs', is the best of this set, but it bears no dedication.

Returning to Russia, the couple stayed at Ivanovka during the summer, where Rachmaninoff began a new composition. This was his first extended work for solo piano, the *Variations on a Theme of Chopin*, Opus 22. The theme is the famous twentieth Prelude in C minor. Rachmaninoff cleverly fuses sonata principle and variation technique in this work, by grouping the variations into a continuous structure which contains the character of a four-movement sonata.

Although Siloti scheduled the Second Concerto for performance in Birmingham and Manchester as well as London during the British tour he was to undertake during 1902, he was beaten to the post for the honour of giving the first British performance by Vladimir Sapellnikov, who premièred the Concerto in Queen's Hall, London, on May 29th. Siloti gave the first performances in the other cities, when in Manchester he appeared in the old Free Trade Hall with the Hallé Orchestra under Hans Richter. The Hallé was possibly the best in Britain then, and the tour was very successful.

Towards the end of 1902, Sergei and Natalia moved into an apartment in the *America* block, and Natalia discovered she was pregnant. Rachmaninoff accepted two undemanding teaching posts, giving him time to pursue his writing and his concert career, which took another step forward with invitations to play the Second Concerto in Vienna and Prague. The performances were to be conducted by Safonoff, whose cool attitude towards Rachmaninoff

Aerial view and interior of the Bayreuth Festival Theatre

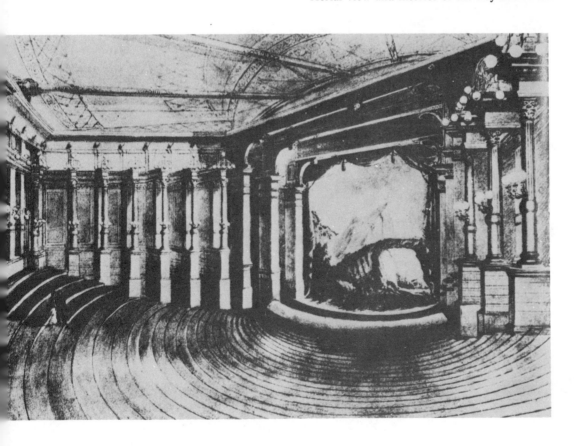

Siloti and Rachmaninoff

Sergei Prokofiev (1891-1953)

continued. Whatever reserve lay between them, the concerts went off smoothly and early in 1903 Rachmaninoff, back in Moscow, gave the first performances of the *Chopin Variations* on February 10th/23rd as well as several of the Opus 23 *Preludes* (the set was incomplete). The G minor, published as Opus 23 No 5, was played then, and became possibly the second favourite of Rachmaninoff's *Preludes*, after the C-sharp minor.

The *Variations* were dedicated to the elderly St Petersburg piano pedagogue, Theodore Leschetizky, whose wife, Annette Essipova, also taught piano at the Conservatory. She had a remarkable pupil joining her class the year following Rachmaninoff's recital, the twelve-year-old Sergei Prokofiev.

While the Rachmaninoffs awaited the birth of their first child, Sergei completed the Opus 23 *Preludes*. As Alexis Weissenberg has pointed out, there is a strong link between them in their published order, so if performed as a set, they make, like Chopin's, an excellent sequence.

Natalia's pregnancy was uncomplicated and a girl, christened Irina, was born on May 14th/27th. No sooner had they gone to Ivanovka for the summer holiday than all three of them fell ill. The parents, themselves unwell, were concerned at the condition of their baby, but after several weeks they all recovered and Rachmaninoff was able to start a major project unfettered by personal worries. This was a new opera, composed with Chaliapin in mind for the title rôle.

The Miserly Knight is one of a series of dramatic poems by Pushkin to be read rather than performed. Rachmaninoff was drawn by the opportunity it afforded him to create a sympathetic part for Chaliapin, and work on *The Miserly Knight* led to him returning to his other postponed opera, *Francesca da Rimini*, which

The Rachmaninoffs' country estate at Ivanovka.

he had started in 1900. He was encouraged by news of first performances of his works abroad: the Cello Sonata, premièred in London on January 18th by Percy Such and Lucy Polgreen in St James's Hall, and in America the First Piano Concerto in Boston, and *The Rock* in New York, by the émigré-formed Russian Symphony Orchestra conducted by Modest Altschuler, an old class-mate of Scriabin and Rachmaninoff, who had emigrated to the U.S.A. some years before.

The Russian government began to reap the whirlwind of Witte's economic policies. The Port Arthur pact with China, which gave Russia access to the Pacific, led to confrontation with Japan, and war broke out on February 6th 1904, eleven days before Puccini's *Madama Butterfly,* set in Japan, received its première at La Scala. The Russian forces were ineffective against the Japanese, and suffered humiliating defeat at Liaotung. The dissident Lenin, whose elder brother had been hanged for his part in an assassination attempt on Alexander III in 1887, watched events from exile in Switzerland.

At home opera dominated Rachmaninoff's life for apart from *The Miserly Knight* and *Francesca* he was invited by the Bolshoi Opera in Moscow to conduct several operas the following season. The Kerzin family, who sponsored concerts under the title 'Friends of Russian Music', also offered Rachmaninoff a contract to conduct a series of orchestral concerts. Alexander Siloti had been musical director of the Bolshoi several seasons previously, and Rachmaninoff's acquaintance with the Tsar's brother, Grand Duke Michael, a music-lover and confidant of the Lievin family, who greatly admired Rachmaninoff's music, doubtless led to the offer to conduct the State Opera. By March 1904 Rachmaninoff completed *The Miserly Knight* and immediately began work on *Francesca da Rimini*, hoping to complete it by the end of his holiday in order to prepare for his début at the Bolshoi in September. In spite of several problems with Modest Tchaikovsky's libretto which were quickly resolved, Rachmaninoff proceeded with the second opera, completing it in August. Early that month he wrote to Modest complaining of a "shortage of words" in the libretto. As the dramaturgical essence of the libretto is weak, Rachmaninoff did not repeat words to flesh out the music, so the libretto's brevity gave rise to problems. However, Rachmaninoff had every reason to feel pleased with the music. He took up his position at the Bolshoi that month and immediately created a sensation at rehearsals.

He was to open with Dargomijsky's *Rusalka* which he had already conducted for the Mamontov Company. He was not to be embarrassed this time. Until Rachmaninoff became musical director it was the custom at the Bolshoi for the conductor to sit close to the stage during performances, with the orchestra behind him. This was fine for the singers, but the orchestra was at a disadvantage in having to follow the conductor from the back. He rearranged the orchestral seating with the approval of Serge Koussevitsky, who recently joined the double-bass section, having completed a five-

Giacomo Puccini (1858-1924)

Sergei Rachmaninoff

Chaliapin in 1900.

year course in the instrument at the Moscow Conservatory in five months! Rachmaninoff's change was sensible and common practice in other opera-houses, but the pampered singers on stage protested. Rachmaninoff had his way, but other conductors during the season had to stand in the old position. He rehearsed the chorus section by section: first the men, the next day the women. In addition, with his superb piano technique and no little experience, he coached the principals at the piano. The changes provoked considerable comment, but they were sensible and necessary: Rachmaninoff criticised the singers frankly, and also the orchestra, but the musicians grew to respect him as they realised his goal was improved standards.

Rusalka opened on September 3rd/16th and was well received. His change of layout brought noticeable improvements: ". . . even in the first bars of the overture the audience began to feel a new freshness and vitality . . ." reported the *Moscovskie Vedomosty* critic Nikolai Kashkin two days later. Rachmaninoff followed this with Tchaikovsky's *Eugene Onegin,* Borodin's *Prince Igor* (with Chaliapin) and also with Chaliapin a centenary production of Glinka's *A Life for the Tsar.* To mark the Glinka centenary, Belaieff founded a series of annual 'Glinka Prizes'. The first were announced that year, and Rachmaninoff received one for his Second Concerto.

This was a busy and successful time for Rachmaninoff: in addition to his opera engagements he had orchestral concerts for the Kerzins. These began shortly after the opera season ended in the spring of 1905 where, among several Russian works, his interpretation of Tchaikovsky's Fifth Symphony won special praise. Nikolai Medtner recalled the performance:

I shall never forget Rachmaninoff's interpretation of Tchaikovsky's Fifth Symphony. Before he conducted it, we heard it only in the version of Nikisch and his imitators . . . his pathetic slowing of the tempo became the law for performing Tchaikovsky, enforced by conductors who had followed him blindly. Suddenly, under Rachmaninoff, all this imitative tradition fell away from the composition and we heard it as if for the first time; especially astonishing was the cataclysmic impetuosity of the finale, an antithesis to the pathos of Nikisch that had always harmed this movement . . .

With the concert and operatic season over Rachmaninoff had cause to feel pleased with his work during the previous eight months, for his undoubted conducting skills in both opera house and concert hall were being recognised at a time when, aged 32, he seemed destined for a great career. However, his compositions demanded his attention and he used all his time during the spring and summer to score the two operas as they were to be produced in a double bill at the Bolshoi during his next season.

The Miserly Knight Opus 24, is dated June 7th/20th, and on July 22nd/August 4th he completed *Francesca da Rimini.* During the early months of the year few Muscovites would have bothered to notice the first performance by Nicholas Richter on February

53

Serge Koussevitzky,
1903.

9th/22nd of a new Piano Sonata composed by the twenty-three-year old Igor Stravinsky. Rachmaninoff doubtless heard that the double-bass player, Serge Koussevitsky, had become engaged to Natalia, daughter of a Moscow tea millionaire.

The young English musician, Leopold Stokowski, was between two stools: he wanted to study conducting under Nikisch in Germany but, as organist and choirmaster of St James's Piccadilly, in London, he received an offer to take up a similar post at St Bartholemew's Church, New York. The church was among the wealthiest in the city, located at the corner of Madison Avenue and 44th street: he decided to go to America, and in September set foot in the New World for the first time.

With the operas written, Rachmaninoff prepared the forthcoming Bolshoi season. Rimsky-Korsakov had completed a new opera, *Pan Voyevoda*, and Rachmaninoff was to conduct the première in September. Rimsky-Korsakov was so impressed with Rachmaninoff's ability during the rehearsals that he invited him to conduct the première of another opera, his recently-completed *The Invisible City of Kitezh*.

Political events, which never bothered Rachmaninoff unduly, now forced themselves to the centre of every stage. The war with Japan went badly for the Russians: Port Arthur fell in January and in March a heavy military defeat at Mukden led to the complete destruction of the Russian fleet at Tsushima on May 27th. This was a catastrophe for the government for the losses (which were territorially very limited) exposed large-scale corruption in high places. Lenin, now in Finland, called the war "the locomotive of revolution". A wave of earlier strikes coincided with the assassination of the Minister of the Interior on July 28th 1904, and several months later street fighting erupted in the capital and Moscow. On January 22nd 1905, a large crowd of workers with their families demonstrated peacefully outside the Winter Palace in St Petersburg, led by Father Gregory Gapon, to present a petition to the Tsar. The guards lost their heads and opened fire: five hundred men, women and children were killed on 'Bloody Sunday', and the wave of revulsion which swept through the country led to the mutiny of the sailors on board the battleship *Potemkin* in June, and strikes in Moscow by printers and railway workers. Almost immediately there was a general strike: even the musicians and the *corps de ballet* at the Bolshoi took part and, alarmed at the turn of events, the Tsar agreed to the main demand of the October manifesto, the founding of the *Duma* (a parliament elected by virtual universal suffrage) under a Prime Minister. Witte, whose capitalist dash for growth had foundered upon the sea of trouble he sought to avoid (war), was named Prime Minister.

For Rachmaninoff, success as an operatic and concert conductor seemed hollow in the face of the worsening political situation. He was preoccupied with other matters. The two operas were premièred on January 11th/24th, 1906, and were repeated four times, but Chaliapin, who Rachmaninoff had in mind when writing the works, did not sing them. Although he appeared the previous season in a revival of *Aleko*, and sight-read the new operas brilliantly at rehearsal, some disagreement or another caused him not to undertake the rôles. Chaliapin's withdrawal from the cast upset Rachmaninoff and relations between the two men remained cool for several months. Nor was this the only casting problem. The original *Francesca*, Antonina Nazhdanova, also withdrew, although she later admitted her action was a "thoughtless, tactless and brainless step". Her successor also withdrew. Rachmaninoff was thus forced to go to another soprano, the forty-three-year old Nadezhda Salina, who sang the rôle to his great satisfaction, but she later said, with disarming candour, that she looked too old for the part.

Although the general strike had ended and work more or less resumed, the militant demands of the Bolshoi staff, including technicians, seamstresses and ushers as well as the musicians, bred dissatisfaction. Rachmaninoff decided to resign at the end of the season. Serge Koussevitsky, in a well-publicised diatribe, also resigned, but he carried little weight. His imminent marriage meant he no longer had to play in the orchestra to earn a living. A revival of Glinka's *A Life for the Tsar* was almost brought to a standstill when lines entreating sacrifice for the Tsar threw the audience into pandemonium, and subsequent performances could only continue with a military contingent in the auditorium. In the St Petersburg Opera performance of *Boris Godunov* the revolution scene had to be deleted, and Rimsky-Korsakov was dismissed from his post at the Conservatory. In protest, Glazunov and Liadov

Revolutionary crowds on Bloody Sunday (9th January 1905) march on the Winter Palace in St Petersburg.

resigned along with others. The Conservatory was closed, and Rimsky-Korsakov took private pupils, among them Igor Stravinsky. In Moscow Taneyev resigned, siding with the pupils against Safonoff's dictatorial methods and reactionary policies. The Moscow Conservatory was also closed, and Safonoff went to America where he became music director of the New York Philharmonic.

It was clear to Rachmaninoff that he could no longer remain in such circumstances. It is also clear from the historical background that his operas stood little chance. With the threat of industrial action, the changes of the casts, and other troubles, it is a wonder the operas managed to be performed at all. Rachmaninoff tended his resignation on the day of the premières but the director, Teliakovsky, managed to persuade him to defer his decision until the end of the season.

The two operas, similar in some respects, differ in others; their playing time (63 minutes) is identical, and the division into three sections is common to both. The vocal writing is rich and characterful (although the libretti makes characterisation difficult) and Rachmaninoff's treatment of the two different subjects is more psychological than descriptive: he shows a deep insight into the motives of the characters, and the orchestral writing is magnificent. Those who doubt Rachmaninoff's ability as an operatic composer should study the orchestration of these works; in this regard it is difficult to name his superior. Rachmaninoff shows a command of his task which is quite outstanding in the early years of the century.

The operas have not entered the standard repertory for reasons which have nothing to do with the worth of the music. In the West, few opera houses perform Russian works; double-bills of short operas almost always mean poor receipts; *The Miserly Knight* demands an all-male cast, which few opera houses can successfully accommodate; *Francesca da Rimini* lacks readily identifiable protagonists, and the chorus parts are sparse — and therefore expensive. Both operas are in their own ways masterpieces, and it is a great pity they are neglected, for Rachmaninoff might easily have become one of this century's greatest operatic composers on the basis of these works. The advance on *Aleko* is startling: if he had had the chance to continue there is no telling what he might have achieved. His sympathy for the voice was inherent; his grasp of orchestral colour was individual and superbly judged; he was an experienced man of the theatre. It is a tragedy that outside events forced him to change direction and anyone who thinks of Rachmaninoff's three operas as curiosities by a composer who was essentially a pianist, had better think again.

After the season ended he decided to leave. Even an offer of the Directorship (although an indication of the esteem in which he was held) failed to disuade him. He decided to take his family abroad for a holiday but during their few months in Italy their sojourn was marred by a recurring illness which struck Irina. However, Rachmaninoff must have been encouraged by the operas, for he wrote to his old friend Slonov requesting his collaboration on a new opera, based on Flaubert's *Salammbo*. He was by all accounts enchanted with Italy, but he expressed concern about his future. He became homesick, and first Natalia and then again Irina fell ill, the child so seriously that he wrote to Morozov:

. . . You cannot imagine how weak she is . . . of that healthy girl only a memory is left. It is hard to describe how we have suffered . . .

Salammbo remained unwritten. Three weeks later Rachmaninoff had had enough: Irina was not improving and their doctor was also due to go abroad. Rachmaninoff learned of the strikes by the Russian railway workers: he doubted they would reach Moscow safely. They decided to go to Ivanovka, away from the troubles, once Irina was better. She recovered completely and at Ivanovka he wrote the fifteen songs Opus 26, which he dedicated to the Kerzins, the sponsors of his orchestral concerts. The Bolshoi again offered a lucrative contract and the Kerzins wanted him for a new concert series. He received a third offer for another orchestral series, but in August Jurgenson told him things were so uncertain no one could guarantee anything. He had to decide, as he received an offer from America as well: he determined to cancel all his Russian engagements, refuse all others, and go abroad for peace and quiet and safety.

6 *Widening Horizons*

In November, 1906, the Rachmaninoff family left Russia for Dresden. Apart from the songs, Opus 26, he had also written that year an *Italian Polka* for piano duet, no doubt as a memento of their Italian visit, which literally became one of his and Natalia's party pieces. Dresden was chosen for a number of reasons. The first was freedom from the troubles in metropolitan Russia; secondly to find a congenial atmosphere which would enable both him to have the relaxed background in which his work could be written and his family could lead a contented life. He heard, or so he disclosed in a letter written shortly after their arrival, that it was not an expensive city, but he complained about the high price of food. The rent of the house they took, a six-roomed two-storey dwelling named Garden Villa on Sidonienstrasse 6, was very reasonable and they settled down quickly and happily. They kept very much to themselves and Rachmaninoff wrote to Slonov:

. . . I work a great deal and I feel very well. In my old age this kind of life pleases me greatly and at present suits me . . .

The reference to "my old age" — he was then thirty-three — has to be taken lightly, of course, but they had been through some trying circumstances in their two years of marriage. No sooner had they arrived in Dresden than Sergei began a number of large-scale compositions which he worked on simultaneously. He also prepared editions of scenes from the two recent operas, which were to be performed in concert version by Chaliapin, with Alexander Siloti conducting. This did much to heal the breach of a year before. Rachmaninoff approached Slonov with a new request for an operatic libretto. After abandoning *Salammbo*, he asked for a text to be fashioned from Maeterlinck's play *Monna Vanna*. This was supplied and he began work immediately, finishing Act I in piano score by April 15th, and drafting ideas for Act II. He had no trouble with this libretto being short on words, as that for *Francesca* had been, for he felt it necessitated shortening. However, he learned the rights for operatic use of Maeterlinck's play had been granted to Henri Février, who had already begun work on his version. Rachmaninoff had no alternative but to postpone all work on the opera.

Two other works began to demand more of his time. The first was a new Symphony in E minor, dedicated to Taneyev, which was drafted by January 1907 and finished in April. A Piano Sonata followed quickly between January and February, the score being completed on May 14th.

He also revised the *Trio Elégiaque* No 2 for a performance in Moscow on February 12th/25th by Goldenweiser with Brandukov and the violinist Carl Grigorovitch, in a concert which also saw the first performance of the Opus 26 songs, with four separate singers (Ivan Grizunov, Anna Kiselovskaya, Alexander Bogdanovitch and Elena Azerskaya) all accompanied by Goldenweiser at a concert sponsored by the dedicatees, the Kerzin family. This was the first occasion Rachmaninoff did not attend the première of one of his works.

The songs form a charming group and are remarkable in the composer's output for their comparative simplicity of expression and epigrammatic utterance. A favourite of Rachmaninoff's "Night is Mournful", was later transcribed for cello and piano at Brandukov's suggestion.

The impressario Serge Diaghilev planned a series of Russian concerts in Paris and Rachmaninoff accepted an invitation to perform his Second Concerto there on May 26th and to conduct "Spring", with Chaliapin singing for the first time the rôle that was written with his voice in mind. After this, the friendship between Rachmaninoff and Chaliapin was completely restored.

The great Russian impressario Serge Diaghilev, founder of the *Ballets Russes.*

During Rachmaninoff's days in Paris he met many Russian friends, including Rimsky-Korsakov and Scriabin, who had recently returned from the United States. Scriabin went to New York at the invitation of his old friend Modest Altschuler, the founder of the Russian Symphony Orchestra in New York. Scriabin was estranged from his wife, and when his mistress Tatiana Schloezer joined him in January he was forced to leave. Safonoff, now director of the New York Philharmonic, was extremely well-connected in New York circles, so when Scriabin had been offhand to Safonoff's wife Vera, he and Tatiana were obliged to leave in a hurry. In Paris Scriabin heard two of his works: the Piano Concerto, played by Josef Hofmann and *The Divine Poem*, both conducted by Arthur Nikisch, who also conducted Rachmaninoff's Concerto. The faithful Altschuler had also performed Rachmaninoff's *Caprice Bohémien* in the United States for the first time, in New York on December 20, 1906, a fortnight after Frances, the last of the Gershvine children, sister to Ira, 'George' and Arthur, was born — ten years to the day after Ira. The concert season in Philadelphia was, as usual, attracting some novelties: Arthur Rubinstein made his début with the orchestra, conducted by Fritz Scheel, in the 1906-07 season.

Natalia was expecting a second child at the end of June 1907: she travelled to Ivanovka to await the birth so Rachmaninoff had to

Rachmaninoff appears to have been a frequent visitor at the home of the Grand Duke Mikhail Alexandrovitch at Brasovo. This photograph, dating from February 1912, shows the composer taking tea with members of the family.

journey to Paris alone. While in Paris he made the acquaintance of Josef Hofmann and he also saw a black-and-white reproduction of a version of Böcklin's *The Isle of the Dead*, a painting which made a deep impression on him. Rachmaninoff's success with the Second Concerto was remarkable. Oskar von Riesemann, who had become friendly with Rachmaninoff in Dresden, and to whom the composer had played the piano Sonata in an unfinished state, described the performance vividly. After his visit to Paris Rachmaninoff was glad to rejoin Natalia at Ivanovka. He was delighted with the lilacs and roses which his sister-in-law Sophia Satina planted at the entrance to the estate. He was certain the child would be a boy, as he wrote to Morozov on June 18th:

. . . First of all, my Natasha, thank God, feels well and is expecting my future son from day to day. The midwife, who has already arrived, waits also. I am waiting, too! In fact all the Ivanovskies are waiting . . . when my son is born, I will let you know . . .

But on June 21st/July 4th, Natalia gave birth to a second daughter, christened Tatiana. Rachmaninoff could now concentrate on preparing the score of the new Symphony which he was to conduct in St Petersburg and Moscow the following January and February. The score was still not quite finished when they returned

60

with their new daughter to Dresden for the winter. The birth of their second child meant a change in the family routine and Rachmaninoff composed no more during 1907. January 1908 was taken up with preparations for the first performance of the Symphony, which he conducted in St Petersburg on January 26th/February 8th, and repeated in Moscow a week later, before conducting a third performance in Warsaw.

Years later, Rachmaninoff agreed to cuts in the Second Symphony, but it is only since the recording made in the USSR in the 1950s, conducted by Alexander Gauk, was released in the West that music-lovers outside Russia have been able to hear the work regularly in its complete, original form. The first movement exposition repeat is still almost always ignored even though it should quite clearly be observed — as should Rachmaninoff's metronome markings. The Second Symphony demands a virtuoso orchestra and conductor but it is frequently performed too slowly, to fatal effect. It is much longer than the First Symphony and plays for about an hour. Such is the surety with which Rachmaninoff handles his vast structure that the work seems not a whit too long. This is not special pleading: it struck its first audiences so. The Moscow critic Yuri Engel, writing after the second performance, remarked:

. . . After listening with unflagging attention to its four movements, one notes with surprise that the hands of the watch have moved sixty-five minutes forward. This may be slightly overlong for the general audience, but how fresh, how beautiful the music is . . .

Like the First, the Second Symphony uses a motto theme but with much greater subtlety (I have to thank Sir Alexander Gibson for revealing to me the extent of Rachmaninoff's genius in this work). It is a great and majestic Symphony, full of power and supremely confident, and displays unusual connections with *The Miserly Knight*. They have the same tonality (E minor — the second scene of the opera is in D minor), and the motto theme of the Symphony clearly derives from a passage towards the end of Act I of the opera. The Symphony is beautifully proportioned, which the later cuts demonstrably do not enhance; beautifully scored, full of the most individual melodies which are fascinatingly worked, it has a breadth and emotional power which set it apart from the music of Rachmaninoff's contemporaries.

Rachmaninoff played the Second Concerto for the first time in England at the Queen's Hall on May 26th, conducted by Serge Koussevitsky who, making his British début, was beginning to show that mastery of orchestral colour and timbre which marked him out as one of the greatest conductors of his day. Koussevitsky had been offered nothing less than a symphony orchestra as a wedding present by his millionaire father-in-law, but he had not yet taken him up on the offer. He was still learning his craft, but he and Rachmaninoff in this performance showed that "freedom from extravagance" which *The Times* critic praised and which was a feature of the subsequent work of both artists (although it had never been a part of Rachmaninoff's make-up). Rachmaninoff missed the British debût of Odessa-born and Leschetizky-trained pianist Benno Moiseiwitsch at Queen's Hall. His return to Russia coincided with the news of the sudden death in St Petersburg of Rimsky-Korsakov aged 64 on June 8th/21st. One more of the 'old guard' had gone. At Ivanovka during the summer Rachmaninoff had time to proof-read the Second Symphony for Gutheil. He also composed a song for the tenth anniversary of the founding of the Moscow Art Theatre entitled "Letter to K.S. Stanislavsky", which Chaliapin sang in Moscow on October 14th/27th, and three days later Konstantin Igumnov gave the first performance of the Piano Sonata Opus 28. Igumnov was a pupil of Pabst and himself became a noted piano teacher, numbering Lev Oborin (who made an early recording of Rachmaninoff's second *Trio Elégiaque* with David Oistrakh and Sviatoslav Knushevitsky), among his pupils. Rachmaninoff missed the première as he had returned to Dresden to prepare for a busy season. Igumnov repeated the Sonata in Leipzig and Berlin, but Rachmaninoff did not hear either performance owing to prior commitments.

Rachmaninoff conducted the Second Symphony for the fourth time in Antwerp (his debût there), and went on to Berlin for a performance of the second *Trio*. He then travelled to Holland for performances of the Second Concerto with Willem Mengelberg and the Concertgebouw Orchestra in Amsterdam and The Hague. Arthur Nikisch surprisingly withdrew the Second Symphony from scheduled performances in Leipzig and Berlin, doubtless slighted at finding, according to Rachmaninoff, that the score was not dedicated to him. However, the worth of the work overcame any petty jealousy, for Nikisch became a noted exponent of the Symphony in later years.

On his return to Dresden just before Christmas, news came from St Petersburg that the Glinka Award Committee had awarded him the major prize in that year's list — the coveted 1,000 roubles — and early in the new year he began work on an orchestral tone-poem suggested by Böcklin's picture *The Isle of the Dead*.

This was the second descriptive work by Rachmaninoff in succession, for the piano Sonata was based on Goethe's *Faust*. The Sonata is conceived on a big scale, like the Second Symphony and the *Chopin Variations,* and there is good reason for linking the three movements (as in Liszt's 'Faust' Symphony) to the characters of Faust, Gretchen and Mephistopheles, but it would be a mistake and a violation of the composer's intentions to read any programme into the work. It is in the favoured key of D minor and the movements, especially the outer ones, have a degree of spaciousness that signals a new voice in his music, comparable only with the vast scale of the Second Symphony. These works together with the First Symphony show Rachmaninoff's ability to write music on the largest scale in a manner that, if one is prepared to give the composer the chance, refutes utterly any lingering notion that he was only capable of writing miniatures.

As the new year dawned he was in Russia for several concerts, which made him miss the première in Dresden on January 25th of Richard Strauss's *Elektra*, but he was doubtless curious to learn of a concert conducted by Siloti in St Petersburg on February 6th/19th which included two new orchestral works by Igor Stravinsky: the twelve-minute *Scherzo Fantastique* Opus 3, and *Fireworks* Opus 4. In the audience, hearing Stravinsky's music for the first time, was Serge Diaghilev, looking for new talent to promote in Paris.

Work on *The Isle of the Dead* continued when the tour ended and the score was completed in Dresden on April 17th, 1909. Rachmaninoff conducted the première in Moscow on April 18th/May 1st (*not* the following day: the calendar difference is confusing).

Dresden is a short journey from Leipzig, where Nikisch was director of the Gewandhaus Orchestra and Rachmaninoff was able to view another version of *The Isle of the Dead* exhibited in a Leipzig gallery. The Swiss artist, Arnold Böcklin died in 1901 aged

Arthur Nikisch with members of the Berlin Philharmonic Orchestra.

63

The Isle of the Dead:
Arnold Böcklin.

29. He painted six versions of this picture, and as Rachmaninoff had been deeply impressed on seeing a copy of one of these versions in Paris, he was curious, on being told of the picture by an acquaintance in Dresden, Nikolai von Struve, to see another.

It is a sombre picture, often dismissed by writers on Rachmaninoff's music, but which is in the opinion of several experts on Germanic art a fine example of its period. Emotionally it occupies a similar world to Schoenberg's *Verklärte Nacht* of 1899, with its unrelieved gloom and deep pessimism. The picture shows a small boat, bearing a coffin placed at right angles, across the River Styx, towards a massive and imposing island, whose gigantic elm-trees dwarf the craft, which is proceeding gently towards a rough-hewn landing-stage contained in a tiny natural harbour. On either side of the island, fashioned from the twin sides of the rock which entombs the trees, are sepulchrous burial-chambers towards which the boat drifts. Even the solitary upright Charon on the boat appears like a shrouded cadaver, albeit the point to which all eyes are inevitably drawn. But its placement, erect and vaguely central, leads one inexorably up towards the trees and round again in a never-ending circular motion. There is rather more to this painting than many music-writers have glimpsed, but it could hardly be described as a great masterpiece. It was well-known at the time, and exerted a powerful fascination on many people. The German composer Max Reger composed a symphonic suite, Opus 128, entitled *Four Tone Poems after Böcklin,* in which the third movement, called *The Isle of the Dead,* is inspired by the same painting. Rachmaninoff's symphonic poem shows once again his

64

mastery of large-scale structures, in an extended movement of vast symphonic proportions. The preoccupation with death, inherent in the title, is not morbid, as in Tchaikovsky's *Pathétique* or Mahler's *Kindertotenlieder,* and its treatment is more objective. It does not sink into hopelessness, and the concluding section, after a finely-judged climax of tremendous passion and force, has an air of calm and gentle repose (musically echoing the opening of the work, but emotionally fulfilling a very different function), consolatory, certainly, but without the self-pity which is the standard emotional state of the typical Romantic. The placement of the *Dies Irae* theme is both logical and masterly, and it is the essentially *civilised* quality of Rachmaninoff's music which has surely guaranteed its survival.

Shortly after the première of *The Isle of the Dead* (his Opus 29) Rachmaninoff was appointed Vice-President of the Imperial Russian Music Society. He took his duties which included responsibility for provincial musical colleges seriously. A more important event now loomed: Rachmaninoff had earlier been approached about a tour in the United States by Henry Wolfsohn, and he had accepted in principle. During the summer holiday at Ivanovka he heard that Wolfsohn had died, and he assumed the plans would fall through, but Mrs Wolfsohn took over her late husband's business. During the negotiations Rachmaninoff worked, in great secrecy as usual, on a new work which he undertook to première in New York. This was the Third Piano Concerto, in D minor, Opus 30. This Concerto was written remarkably quickly and he looked forward to at least one benefit from the tour, the purchase of a motor car, even though the prospect of the gruelling itinerary did not fill him with joy.

In spite of his doubts concerning the trip he arrived in the United States at the end of October, taking with him the score of the new Concerto. Modest Altschuler met him at the dockside. As it had only been finished on September 23rd/October 6th, there was no time for the Concerto to be printed, so the scheduled performances had to be given from the manuscript. It was a formidable tour: the Wolfsohns had arranged twenty concerts in and around the important cities of the north-eastern USA, and in view of the tightness of the schedule Rachmaninoff practised assiduously on a dummy keyboard during the Atlantic crossing. His American debût was a recital in Smith College, Northampton, in Hampshire County, Massachusetts, on November 4th. Northampton is a small town 160 miles north-east of New York City, from where he went to Boston to play the Second Concerto with the Boston Symphony Orchestra under Max Fiedler (no relation to Arthur — who, although born in Boston, his father Isaac being a member of the orchestra at this time, was preparing to go to Berlin for five years' study in 1910). He also played the Concerto with the Boston Symphony and Fiedler in Baltimore and New York. He stayed in New York to prepare for the most important event of the tour: the première of the new Concerto which was to be given on November

28th with the New York Symphony Orchestra, conducted by Walter Damrosch, in the New Theatre Manhattan. Two days later they repeated the work at Carnegie Hall, but for many people the most important performance of the work was the third, given by the New York Philharmonic Orchestra, under its recently-appointed musical director, Gustav Mahler, Safonoff's successor. This took place on January 16th, 1910, also at Carnegie Hall.

The critics as well as the public therefore had a rare triple chance to hear the new work. The press reaction was distinctly cool, unlike that of the audiences who knew a great work when they heard one. Following the first performance, on the Sunday afternoon, the *New York Herald* reported:

... Mr Rachmaninoff was recalled several times in the determined effort of the audience to make him play again, but he held up his hands with a gesture which meant that although he was willing, his fingers were not. So the audience laughed and let him retire ...

The critics were not so easily carried away. The main reviews, in the *Herald*, the New York *Sun* and the New York *Daily Tribune* all complained about the work's length.

They were nevertheless unanimous in declaring the Concerto to be a landmark in Rachmaninoff's career. The Concerto's length was a cause of concern to Rachmaninoff himself, but in this work he achieved in concerto form what he had created in symphony, symphonic poem and sonata: a great instrumental work on the largest scale. Longer than the Second Concerto, the degree of integration of thematic ideas and the more proliferating solo part mark this out as a concerto of rare quality. The first movement is a daring and highly successful formal innovation: after the two main themes — both given to the piano (for the first time in any of his concertos) — an immense two-pronged development section follows. The first is with orchestra, but the second is the cadenza, the longest and most difficult in these works. The structure of this movement is thus delicately poised, and a curious point is that, for the first half of the cadenza, Rachmaninoff wrote two versions, both quite different pianistic treatments of the material. What they share equally is tremendous drive and energy.

The slow movement is a set of variations on a theme derived from the first subject of the first movement, and includes a fantastic *scherzando* section, after the manner of the Second Concerto, but much more intricate and cleverly-worked. It is often pointed out that the clarinet tune in this section is the opening theme of the concerto, note for note, but in a different key, the major mode, and varied with much syncopation. What is not so generally realised is that the piano figuration which weaves a scintillating arabesque around the theme is itself an immensely speeded-up version of the theme as well. The finale is heroic and cossack-like, but contains a succession of *tableaux* which combine a variety of mood within the same basic tempo, and this variety can seem a little long if the soloist does not judge the movement accurately. There are many

Rachmaninoff in New York at the time of his first visit to the USA in 1909.

pianists who know the notes of this marvellous work, but few who have grasped the musical meaning of this difficult finale.

Shortly after the first New York performances, Rachmaninoff toured several states as conductor. The young Leopold Stokowski had been invited to return to the USA as conductor of the Cincinatti Orchestra (following a period of study in Europe with Nikisch, after leaving St. Bartholemew's, and his début as an orchestral conductor in Paris), and Rachmaninoff made his first appearance with Stokowski later in the tour. He appeared first with the Philadelphia Orchestra, commencing an association which was to last over thirty years. No one could forsee that Rachmaninoff's first concert began a long relationship, or that 500 miles due West, in Cincinatti, Stokowski was to play a vital part in it.

It was the Philadelphia Orchestra that gave the first American performance of Rachmaninoff's Second Symphony, and from the City of Brotherly Love Rachmaninoff travelled to Chicago where he directed the Theodore Thomas Orchestra in the Second Symphony and the American première of *The Isle of the Dead*, repeating the symphonic poem with the Boston Symphony Orchestra. His tremendous musicianship as composer, conductor and pianist, impressed musicians everywhere, especially in Boston, where he was offered the conductorship. The recently-formed Boston Opera Company, a direct rival to the Metropolitan, which boasted several Russian principals from the Bolshoi among its newly-acquired artists, planned the United States première of Rachmaninoff's *The Miserly Knight* the following year. But the thought of leaving Russia for good was unbearable. He played the Second Concerto with the Chicago Orchestra under Frederick Stock. His piano recitals were made up in large part of his own works.

Towards the end of the tour, the third performance of the Third Concerto took place in New York under Mahler, and later Rachmaninoff recalled the performance. The rehearsal was remarkable for Mahler's tenacity:

. . . The rehearsal began at ten o'clock. I was to join it at eleven, and arrived in good time. But we did not begin work until twelve, when there was only half an hour left . . . we played and played . . . half an hour was long past, but Mahler did not pay the slightest attention to this fact.

Forty-five minutes later Mahler announced: 'Now we will repeat the first movement'. My heart froze within me. I expected a dreadful row, or at least, a heated protest from the orchestra. This would certainly have happened with any other orchestra, but here I did not notice a single sign of displeasure. The musicians played the first movement with a keen or perhaps even closer application than the previous time. At last, we had finished. I went up to the conductor's desk, and together we examined the score. The musicians in the back seats began quietly to pack up their instruments and to disappear. Mahler blew up: 'What is the meaning of this?'

'It is half-past one, Maestro.'

'That makes no difference! As long as I'm sitting, no musician has a right to get up!'

67

It must have been a memorable performance, for Rachmaninoff admired Mahler greatly, particularly his insistence on rehearsing the orchestral accompaniment to the point of perfection. As both were great composers as well as great conductors, it was a rare meeting of musical minds: Rachmaninoff was very impressed with Mahler's interpretation of Berlioz's *Symphonie Fantastique*, which concluded the concert.

The tour was a complete artistic and financial success, so much so that he was offered, in addition to the Boston Symphony appointment, a more extensive tour the following season. But he was homesick and turned a deaf ear to all entreaties. Homesickness aside, he was immensely proud of the success he enjoyed everywhere on the tour; he was assured of a warm welcome should he decide to return. When it was over, in March, he returned to Russia, where he premièred the Third Concerto on April 4th/17th in Moscow, conducted by Eugene Plotnikov (which at one point was in jeopardy as the orchestral parts went astray en route from New York, but they turned up in time). Russian critics did not share the American view of the Concerto's length: Grigor Prokofiev, writing in *Russkiye Vedomosti*, spoke of the 'sharp and laconic form'.

Shortly after Rachmaninoff's return Balakirev, founder of 'The Five' fifty years before, died aged 73. Two English performances in the spring would have delighted Sergei: on February 23rd, the student orchestra of the Royal College of Music gave the British première of *The Isle of the Dead*, conducted by Sir Charles Stanford, and Arthur Nikisch gave the Second Symphony for the first time in that country at the Queen's Hall on May 19th under the patronage of the Royal Philharmonic Society. The concert took place on the eve of the funeral of King Edward VII who died on May 6th.

At one of the last concerts of his Russian season Rachmaninoff received a bouquet of white lilacs from a female admirer, who signed the accompanying card "The White Lilac Lady". It is not unusual for artists to attract wellwishers, but this lady, whom he never met, sent a bouquet of white lilacs, whatever the season, to all his concerts, even those abroad. It was many years later that he learned her identity, through his sister-in-law, Sophia Satina. She was Madame Fekla Rousseau. Once the concerts in Russia were over Rachmaninoff rejoined his family for a well-earned holiday at Ivanovka. He had become owner of the estate, and he took his duties seriously. The farming and horse-riding, however, enabled him to relax completely with his wife and children after his strenuous concert-tours, and during the next few years he reinvested most of the residue from his concerts into developing the estate. Although the estate kept Rachmaninoff busier than usual (even though during the previous summers he had gradually come to take a large share in running it) this must have been a particularly happy time, for he managed to compose two works including his first extended sacred piece, a setting of the *Liturgy of St John Chrysostom* Opus 31. This was written for large unaccompanied mixed choir, as musical instruments, even the organ, were forbidden in Russian churches under the strict rules of the Orthodox Church. In services the main choir was often echoed by a small choir placed apart, sometimes comprising solo singers. The antiphonal result produces, in Russian Orthodox Church music, a distinctive tone-quality and timbre which had already commended itself to non-believing composers. It is therefore not strange that Rachmaninoff should have composed this work even though, as on the occasion of his marriage, he was rather indifferent to Orthodox religion. The *Liturgy* is probably the most frequently celebrated in the Russian Orthodox Church, and shortly after it was completed (July 30th/August 12th) Rachmaninoff wrote to Morozov:

. . . I have finished only the *Liturgy* (to your great surprise). I have been thinking about the *Liturgy* for a long time and for a long time I was striving to write it. I started work on it somehow by chance and then suddenly became fascinated with it. And then I finished it very quickly. Not for a long time (since my work on *Monna Vanna)* have I written anything with such pleasure. That is all . . .

Rachmaninoff's reference to *Monna Vanna* is interesting: he evidently considered it still on the stocks, awaiting the appearance of Février's setting (which was imminent). It was the only unfinished manuscript he took with him when he finally left Russia. Rachmaninoff was very busy at this time with his largest group of *Preludes,* the thirteen which comprise Opus 32. With them, he completed a set of twenty-four *Preludes* in each key (including the C-sharp minor and the ten of Opus 23). A subtle point occurs in the final *Prelude,* the D flat major. This is the enharmonic major of the first *Prelude,* the C-sharp minor, and the D-flat *Prelude* transforms material from the earlier piece. The Opus 32 set was written between August 23rd/September 10th/23rd, a remarkably short time. As three of them (Nos 5, 11 and 12) were written on the same day, Rachmaninoff's inspiration was running high. He was also preparing for the forthcoming concert season, for earlier in the year, after his return from the United States, he accepted the position of conductor of the Moscow Philharmonic Concerts. This appointment lasted for three seasons, and his programmes were notable for their range of sympathies: his own music featured, naturally, but during his directorship he conducted works by Elgar, Debussy, Scriabin, Richard Strauss, Berlioz, Brahms, Mozart, Beethoven, Wagner and many other composers, including Glazunov, not letting the debâcle of the First Symphony's premiere affect his programme-planning. He also toured Russia and abroad as a pianist, which had to be fitted in to his conducting duties. Starting with the 1910-11 season Rachmaninoff became, within three years, the leading conductor in Russia, until the rise to prominence of Serge Koussevitsky.

In the spring of 1911 Rachmaninoff heard the news from Vienna of the death of Gustav Mahler on May 18th. Mahler, who was 50, conducted his final New York Philharmonic concert on February

21st (his Fourth Symphony for the last time on January 18th) but by then it was clear the heart condition from which he suffered, since it was diagnosed in 1907, was so advanced that he had little time to live. Shortly before Mahler's death, Rachmaninoff wrote a lively *Polka de V.R.* for piano (the V.R. being his father, Vasily Rachmaninoff). It is uncertain when his father wrote the tune, but it could have been one described by one of Sergei's aunts, when she recalled Vasily ". . . spent hours playing the piano, not the well-known pieces, but something — God knows what . . . but I listened to the end." The Polka is dated March 11th/24th, and dedicated to Leopold Godowsky. It was in the late summer that Rachmaninoff, as usual with his family at Ivanovka, began a new series of piano pieces, whose title, *Etudes-Tableaux*, indicates pictorial inspiration, although, replying to a question later in life, he said, "I do not believe in the artist disclosing too much of his images. Let them paint for themselves what they most suggest." When Respighi orchestrated several *Etudes-Tableaux* in 1930, Rachmaninoff supplied him with programmes as a guide, but they seem far-fetched, one of the later set allegedly depicting Little Red Riding Hood's visit to Granny.

However, there is evidence to suggest Rachmaninoff composed these works to illustrate childhood scenes for his two young children to hear (certainly not to play! — they are among his most virtuosic pieces). Rachmaninoff wrote nine *Etudes-Tableaux*, but he was uncertain about their order: he withdrew three when they came to be published in 1914. Later he refashioned the original No.4 as one of a second set, but the others remained unpublished until after his death. The original order is now restored, but there is some justification for believing the first publication is better: heard as a set of six, as originally published, there is greater cohesion than in the now usually heard set of eight.

Gustav Mahler, 1860-1911.

Shortly after completing these virtuoso studies, Rachmaninoff began another heavy season, including an English tour. On October 24th, 1911, he gave the English première of the Third Concerto in Liverpool, with the Philharmonic conducted by Simon Speelman. The first London performance came on November 7th, in the Queen's Hall, at a Royal Philharmonic Society Concert, conducted by his friend and collaborator, Willem Mengelberg. Thirteen days later, in Munich, Bruno Walter conducted the posthumous première of Mahler's *Das Lied von der Erde* with Madame Charles Cahlier and William Miller.

By then Rachmaninoff was back in Russia preparing his conducting season with the Moscow Philharmonic. Events had worsened in Russia with the assassination, on September 11th, of Prime Minister Stolypin, who had succeeded Witte as Prime Minister in 1906, sitting in a box in a theatre in Kiev. Reaction followed, and the agrarian reform which Stolypin instigated was effectively reduced by the poorly-led *Dumas* which followed. The Empress, concerned for her haemophiliac son, the Tsarevitch, became influenced more and more by the notorious Rasputin. She came to

70

regard this uneducated self-seeker as God's chosen instrument. Rasputin's influence on the Royal Family, and through them, political life, was quite insidious, as the Tsar was anxious not to upset his wife who he felt had suffered enough over their son. Rasputin's influence became a national scandal, and he came to epitomise all that was wrong with the ruling system.

Rachmaninoff had rather more pressing worries. Serge Koussevitsky had returned to Moscow following a successful European tour, during which he established himself as a conductor of great ability; also, through the music publishing house he founded, a shrewd entrepreneur. He established his own orchestra and announced a season of concerts. Koussevitsky's programmes were generally more *avant-garde* than Rachmaninoff's and he set himself up as the champion of modernism, especially promoting the music of Scriabin. Newspapers love public quarrels and although Rachmaninoff had no desire to become involved in one, his position made him an unwilling rival of Koussevitsky.

However, for those who were above this manufactured rivalry, the season brought consolation: a performance of Tchaikovsky's First Piano Concerto, with Rachmaninoff playing the solo and Alexander Siloti conducting, was one, and for Rachmaninoff the early months of 1912 saw an element enter his life which remained something of a mystery until after his death. A letter from a lady who cryptically signed herself "Re" caught his attention. He replied, and an acquaintance developed which lasted until 1917. The correspondence is unusual, for Rachmaninoff used his replies to the lady (whom he learned was a young poetess, Marietta Shaginian) as an outlet for a deeper and more contemplative train of thought than he used in correspondence with others.

Rachmaninoff was glad to have this outlet, as he was unwilling to drag his family into the conflicts and so disturb the home atmosphere. Marietta Shaginian was a remarkable young lady, for after the revolution in 1917, she became one of Russia's most important authoresses. She not only befriended Rachmaninoff, but also the Medtners, and in her preface to the Rachmaninoff letters she published after his death, gave a pen-portrait of the musician she knew which shows her sympathies and literary skill. Their relationship was purely platonic, but Rachmaninoff was undoubtedly refreshed by the understanding support of the young lady at a particularly trying time. The portrait of her, painted in 1911 by Tatiana Hyppius, shows a young woman whose facial characteristics reflect her Armenian pedigree. Marietta Shaginian was a liberal-minded intellectual, like many of her generation and background (her father, Sergei Shaginian, was a professor at the Moscow University) and she had already published articles on art, literature and music. She recalled later:

... In February 1912, such a snow storm was raging that one felt lost even in the centre of the city. One felt as though one were swept on to the Russian Steppes, into Pushkin's *Snow Storm*. It was during one of these February nights that I wrote a letter to Sergei Rachmaninoff, whom I did not know at the time. I sent my

71

Marietta Shaginian — a portrait painted in 1911 by Tatiana Hyppius.

letter to catch him in St Petersburg, where he had gone for a concert, and I signed it "Re" to conceal my real name. Later on, even up to the last days of our friendship (which lasted from February 1912 to July 1917) I remained "Re" for him. He never called me anything else . . .

Rachmaninoff's attention may well have been caught by the signature "Re" — in French, the musical note D, the key which symbolised so much in his music, including now, of course, the Third Concerto. Their correspondence quickly developed, and her literary knowledge soon proved invaluable to the composer, for by March he wrote asking for help in selecting texts for songs:

. . . So long as the piece is original and not translated and not longer than eight or twelve-sixteen lines at the maximum. And here is something else. The mood

72

should be sad rather than happy. The light, happy, colours do not come easily to me . . .

Rachmaninoff was now troubled by the Russian Musical Society, of which he was Vice-President. A dispute over policy led to his resignation in support of Pressman, who had been dismissed. Although things were temporarily patched up, he resigned again, finally, on May 28th/June 10th, and free at last of this call on his time, he settled down to the composition of the songs. He wrote (or revised from earlier drafts) thirteen songs between June 4th/17th and June 19th/July 2nd. The fourteenth, the *Vocalise*, was written the previous April.

Politically, events moved with unrelenting certainty. The reactionary forces who replaced the assassinated Stolypin, found their policies failing disastrously: the people refused further oppression after having experienced a measure of liberty. In Irkutsk, Siberia, at the Lean goldmine, the miners came out on strike. As their strike had a direct effect on the economy, troops were called in to force them to return: 107 miners were shot dead on April 18th. Widespread strikes followed the massacre, and during the second conference of the Russian Social Democratic Worker's Party in Prague, the Mensheviks were driven out and the Bolsheviks forged into a cohesive party.

These happenings did little to disturb the summer at Ivanovka, a principal event of which was the delivery of Rachmaninoff's first car. Motor vehicles outside the larger Russian cities were extremely rare and, after one or two teething troubles, Rachmaninoff soon got a big kick out of driving it himself, even though he engaged a chauffeur. He found the exhilaration of motoring in the country with the hood down (it was a large — and expensive — coupé) a great relaxation, and a photograph taken at the time shows the proud owner at the wheel with the chauffeur (correctly uniformed, of course) at his side.

The new season marked a number of significant events: the Bolshoi revived Rachmaninoff's *Francesca da Rimini*, without *The Miserly Knight*, but the revival did not establish a repertory place for the work (it was not revived at the Bolshoi until 1956). Rachmaninoff's season opened on October 6th/19th with a Moscow Philharmonic Concert, but he cancelled a St Petersburg concert to play Tchaikovsky's First Concerto, owing to stiffness in his fingers. His conducting was not affected, even though it was strenuous, until the last date which he also cancelled, suffering from overwork and exhaustion. He had given eleven orchestral concerts in two months, and their preparation, to say nothing of the worsening political situation, fatigued him. The running battle in the press also distressed him. As before, at the Bolshoi season of 1905-06, Rachmaninoff felt the need to get away: the concert season had proved almost too much (the preparation for his performances of Berlioz's *Symphonie Fantastique* especially). He needed rest and time to compose, and he wrote to Marietta Shaginian on November 12th/25th replying to her complaint he had ignored her:

The composer driving his first motor car, with his chauffeur as passenger, at Ivanovka

73

... If I do not answer your letters promptly, it is only because of my large correspondence and all sorts of business ... I am just tired, very tired, and I live on my last ounces of strength. At the concert yesterday, for the first time in my life, on one of the *fermate* I forgot what to do next and to the great distress of the whole orchestra I tried for a long time to remember what was coming next. I wish to God I could leave soon ...

To an artist of Rachmaninoff's integrity, such a lapse was unpardonable: he took his family abroad, after his last-but-one orchestral concert on December 1st/9th. They left on December 5th/18th, and stayed a week in Berlin, before deciding to leave for Switzerland, where they spent a month. Rachmaninoff recovered his strength so much so that when they travelled on to Rome he wrote to Marietta on March 23rd saying he was working very hard, but another serious worry pushed all thoughts of composition aside. As on their previous Italian trip, illness struck again. Both daughters went down with typhoid, and Rachmaninoff, alarmed at their condition, took them back to Berlin for treatment: Tatiana was admitted to hospital, on the danger list. After some time, both children improved sufficiently for them to travel to Ivanovka, where they recovered completely.

Back at his summer home, Rachmaninoff was able to complete the work begun in Rome, curiously enough in the same flat on the Piazza di Spagna that Modest Tchaikovsky once occupied. This was his 'choral symphony' (not numbered, and not so called by Rachmaninoff), for soloists, chorus and orchestra: *The Bells*, Opus 35 to a Russian translation by Balmont of Edgar Allan Poe's poem. The impetus for the choral work had come, anonymously, from a young pupil of Mikhail Bukinik, a cellist Maria Danilova, an admirer of Rachmaninoff. The four movements of *The Bells* were completed in full score on July 27th/August 9th, and dedicated to "my friend Willem Mengelberg and his orchestra in Amsterdam", but it was Rachmaninoff himself, not Mengelberg, who conducted the first performance, in St Petersburg on November 30th/December 13th, with Popova, Alexandrov and Andreyev as soloists, with the Chorus of the Maryinsky Theatre, after which he embarked on an English tour.

The Bells was Rachmaninoff's favourite work. It is the biggest of his choral-orchestral works, scored for a very large orchestra (including quadruple woodwind, six horns, much percussion with piano, harp, celesta and optional organ). The thematic integration is on a very high level and the imaginative treatment of the text gives each movement a clearly defined character. Poe's verses formally parallel a four-movement symphony, and also constitute a mirror of life: the first movement, "The Silver Sleigh Bells" is an evocation of childhood; the second, "The Mellow Wedding Bells" makes a tender slow movement; the third, "The Loud Alarm Bells" forms a fantastic scherzo, and the finale, "The Mournful Iron Bells", a slow movement of death. This means, of course, that the work ends with a slow movement, which is lugubrious but ultimately consolatory. In many ways, *The Bells* is a counterpart to

The composer with his first automobile, 1912

The Maryinsky Theatre in St. Petersburg

Manuscript page of *Monna Vanna*

Tchaikovsky's *Pathétique* Symphony (which also ends with a slow movement) and Mahler's *Das Lied von der Erde*.

Three days after the première of *The Bells*, Rachmaninoff returned to Moscow to give the première of the new Second Piano Sonata on December 3rd/16th. It was dedicated to Pressman. Although Rachmaninoff later revised the choral parts of *The Bells*'s scherzo (not necessarily an improvement: another example of Rachmaninoff's first thoughts being better) the Second Sonata caused great difficulty.

Rachmaninoff was interested in the production of the Boston Opera Company of his *The Miserly Knight*, but he would have been chagrined at the reports of Février's *Monna Vanna*, which the Company premièred on December 4th, 1913. *The Monthly Musical Record* for April 1914 dismissed it as "rather undistinguished". Now that Février's piece had appeared, the way was open for Rachmaninoff to proceed with his *Monna Vanna*.

Shortly after the premières of *The Bells* and the Second Sonata, in January 1914 Rachmaninoff travelled to England for another tour. He gave the Second Sonata in Bradford on January 30th, and while in Yorkshire he agreed that *The Bells* should have its British première at the Sheffield Festival later that year, but events intervened.

Back in Moscow, he introduced *The Bells* on February 8th/21st. The tremendous success of the performance was complete: for Rachmaninoff, the reception was almost gladiatorial. Laurel wreaths, flowers and gifts were heaped upon him by the audience as part of a tremendous public display of affection and admiration. It was the greatest triumph of his career.

7 War

By the summer of 1914, the international situation had become full of menace. The Balkan Wars of 1912 and 1913 saw the major powers lining up behind the smaller combatants, and although peace came fitfully in 1913 Bosnia, for example, still remained under Austrian control. The assassination of Archduke Franz Ferdinand and his wife the Duchess of Hohenberg, heirs to the Austrian throne, during a visit to Sarajevo, the Bosnian capital, set off a chain of events which led to the outbreak of war throughout Europe. Austria issued an ultimatum to Bosnia, but the Tsar's government intervened claiming that the action was an oblique challenge to Russia. Germany counter-acted, in turn, siding with Austria: an ultimatum was issued to Russia. When this expired, Germany declared war on August 1st. By August 4th, France, Belgium and Great Britain were at war with Germany.

After the outbreak of hostilities Rachmaninoff cut short his holiday. The family went to his brother-in-law's estate in the Urals, far from the fighting. Rachmaninoff was very concerned, remembering the unrest which followed the Russian defeat by the Japanese, but the successful defence of St Petersburg by the Russian army encouraged him back to Moscow. Another of the 'old guard', Liadov, died aged 59 on August 15th/28th, and Rachmaninoff conducted a memorial concert of Liadov's works concluding with his own Second Symphony.

The contrived rivalry between Rachmaninoff and Koussevitsky was forgotten when they toured Southern Russia together in aid of the war effort. The concert tours, the war, and the demands of the estate conspired to prevent Rachmaninoff composing during 1914, but music was welling up inside him: an authority on medieval church music, Stepan Smolensky, whom Rachmaninoff knew, died in 1914. Between January and February 1915 Rachmaninoff composed another masterpiece, which he dedicated to Smolensky's memory. This was the *Vesper Mass, 'Night Vigil'* (*Vsenoshchnoye bdeniye*), Opus 37.

In many ways, the *Night Vigil* is the most remarkable work Rachmaninoff wrote. Written for large unaccompanied choir, in the manner of the Opus 31 *Liturgy*, it is conceived on a vast and

Alexander Nikolayevitch
Scriabin, 1872-1915.

spacious scale. Profoundly uplifting in character, it is brilliant, like the interior of a great cathedral, drenched in sunlight, with the sun's beams shining through massive stained-glass windows, flooding the altar and interior with a blaze of natural luminescence. Rachmaninoff's use of the choir is full of the most subtle and finely-judged light and shade. His thematic material is based largely on traditional Orthodox chants, but handled with a sureness and individuality that finally dispels any hoary ideas about Rachmaninoff's lack of artistry. This great masterpiece, for such it is, demonstrates yet another facet of this superb creative musician's nature.

The first performance was given in Moscow by the Synodical Choir conducted by Nikolai Danilin at a war charity concert on March 10th/23rd. It made, as it has always done, a most profound impression and four further performances followed soon after. An appreciation which touched Rachmaninoff deeply was that expressed by his old professor Taneyev. At that time the musical world was shocked by the sudden death at the age of 43, of Scriabin. Rachmaninoff and Koussevitsky collaborated in a series of concerts in his memory. At one of these Rachmininoff played Scriabin's Piano Concerto with Koussevitsky conducting and, at a solo recital, Scriabin's Fifth Sonata. In the audience was Prokofiev, then 24, to whom Scriabin was a musical hero. Shortly before his death, on a visit to Kiev, Scriabin had heard a remarkable ten-year-old pianist from that city, Vladimir Horowitz, whose parents sought Scriabin's advice. His only suggestion was that they offer their son an environment of culture and artistry in which he could develop beyond pianism.

Rachmaninoff's recitals were not purely artistic endeavours: the proceeds were donated to Scriabin's dependants, but Rachmaninoff's interpretations were not to the liking of the young 'Scriabinists' who made their displeasure known. After the recital Rachmaninoff saw Prokofiev (whom he had met previously, when their conversation was amicable) who, with some tactlessness, said: "Nonetheless, Sergei Vasilievitch, I think you played it very well." Rachmaninoff replied, "Did you think I would play it badly, then?", and turned his back on Prokofiev. That incident, wrote Prokofiev, "ended our good relations."

Another sad occasion quickly followed when Taneyev, a mourner at Scriabin's funeral, caught a chill at the graveside and, less than two months later, succumbed to the complications which developed. The Rachmaninoffs heard of his death in Finland, where they were staying with Alexander Siloti's family. The obituary Rachmaninoff wrote, quoted in Chapter 3, eloquently shows his veneration for his old professor.

There were, however, some bright spots in the summer months: Rachmaninoff had met a rising young soprano Nina Koshetz (whose father had been a bass principal at the Bolshoi, but committed suicide in 1904), and her artistry impressed him greatly. She was then twenty years old, had graduated from the Moscow

The composer c.1914.

With Chaliapin, 1916.

Conservatory in 1912 as a pianist, playing a Rachmaninoff Concerto at her graduation concert. She went to Paris to study singing with Felicia Litvinne, the dedicatee of Rachmaninoff's song, "Dissonance" (incidentally, Litvinne took part in Leopold Stokowski's conducting début in Paris in 1909). At short notice on her return from Paris she deputised to sing the *Liebestod* from Wagner's *Tristan und Isolde,* and this led to further engagements.

Rachmaninoff and Koshetz met again at a Taneyev memorial concert. From England came news of two performances: in July, Vladimir Rosing's Russian Opera Company successfully premièred *Aleko* at the London Opera House. Goureivitch conducted and Melisand d'Egville sang Zemfira. The indefatigable Henry J. Wood (knighted after his wife's death in 1909) gave the professional première of *The Isle of the Dead* at a Queen's Hall Promenade Concert on August 25th. Apart from revising the *Vocalise* from Opus 34, Rachmaninoff only wrote a fragment from St John's Gospel for a war relief publication the previous February 16th/March 1st.

A highlight of the new season (and another demonstration of the lack of animosity between Rachmaninoff and Koussevitsky) was an all-Rachmaninoff concert conducted by Koussevitsky comprising *Spring,* the Third Concerto (with Rachmaninoff as soloist) and *The Bells.* After Gutheil's death some months before, Koussevitsky's music publishing firm had taken over the Gutheil catalogue, which effectively made Koussevitsky Rachmaninoff's publisher (apart from those works published by Jurgenson) and Koussevitsky contracted to publish Rachmaninoff's later works. Rachmaninoff, together with Oskar von Riesemann and Nikolai von Struve, joined the board of Koussevitsky's German company some years before the outbreak of the war in an advisory capacity: he had no say in the running of the parent company in Russia. The first work published under the new arrangement was the *Night Vigil.* Early in 1916 Rachmaninoff again met Nina Koshetz and, having asked Marietta Shaginian for a selection of poems, he decided to compose some songs for the soprano (his nearest approach to a song-cycle) and perform them during the 1916/17 season. While recuperating from the concert season at the Caucasian resort of Essentuki, Rachmaninoff heard of his father's death at Ivanovka. Vasily had intended to join Sergei's family for the summer, but he died while they were away for a few weeks.

The war continued relentlessly. In February 1916 the Germans attacked Verdun; at the end of May a decisive naval battle between the British and German fleets took place off the coast of Jutland. A german submarine, the *Deutschland,* actually reached the coast of the United States at Norfolk, Virginia, on July 9th, at the height of the first battle of the Somme, and the sinking of the *Lusitania* gave rise to enormous anti-German feeling in America. Although many American immigrants had fled Europe to seek life afresh in the New World, events were leading to an inevitable USA involvement in the conflict.

The young Leopold
Stokowski *Photo: RCA*.

As far as music in America was concerned the event of the 1915-16 season was the United States première of Mahler's Eighth Symphony by the Philadelphia Orchestra under Leopold Stokowski. After several seasons with the Cincinatti Orchestra, he had been appointed conductor of the Philadelphia Orchestra, quickly making a considerable reputation for adventurous programmes (he programmed *Das Lied von der Erde*, and had introduced Elgar's Second Symphony to the USA in Cincinatti, shortly after its London première). His German studies were invaluable, since German was the only language spoken at rehearsals of the orchestra for some time after his arrival.

Later in 1916 the inventor of the Ampico Piano Roll system, Charles Fuller Stoddard, demonstrated it at the Hotel Biltmore in New York City. Whilst staying in Germany before the war Rachmaninoff was approached with a view to making some piano rolls and he cut several, including parts of the Second Concerto. Whether they were issued commercially is uncertain. The worsening political situation possibly prevented their release: none have survived. By the summer of 1916, apart from the two songs Rachmaninoff had composed nothing since the *Night Vigil* of February 1915 but, with his family safely back at Ivanovka and recovered from his father's death, he settled down to writing the songs for Nina Koshetz. Marietta Shaginian sent a group of contemporary poems whose symbolism, quite different from anything he had attempted before, led him to adopt a freer style. The cream of this set composed mainly in September 1916 are 'Daisies'

(No 3) and 'The Dream' (No 5), which is curiously dated November 2nd/15th after the first performance of the group on October 24th/November 6th given, naturally, by Nina Koshetz and Rachmaninoff. By then Rachmaninoff had already completed another work, the second set of *Etudes-Tableaux* for solo piano, Opus 39. The first four followed immediately after the songs, and to these Rachmaninoff added a revision of the withdrawn A minor from the otiginal Opus 33. On November 29th in St Petersburg (now renamed Petrograd since 1914), Rachmaninoff played the first four of these *Etudes-Tableaux*. Together with the revisions of the discarded Opus 33 pieces and those written by the following February, the nine published studies form the complete Opus 39. They mark a distinct development in Rachmaninoff's career: tonally, they are more fluid, resembling the chromaticism of Scriabin expressed within staggeringly difficult virtuoso writing. Like the first set, pictorial images are the basis for several of them: the first, in C major was suggested by another Böcklin painting, *The Waves*, and includes a reference to the *Dies Irae*. This plain-chant forms the basis for the second piece, also being heard in the third, fourth, fifth and seventh of the studies. The eighth, in D minor, was inspired by Bocklin's painting *Morning*. Finally, the ninth, D major, contains an uneasy rhythm which suggests a literary background, particularly with its *Tempo di marcia* indication.

The complete Opus 39 was premièred in Petrograd on February 21st/March 6th 1917 by Rachmaninoff. Rumours spread concerning Rachmaninoff and Nina Koshetz and, shortly after, Rachmaninoff felt that their collaboration should cease. Both families had heard the gossip, which was doubtless without foundation, but to Rachmaninoff proper artistic collaboration could not flourish in such an atmosphere.

By the beginning of 1917 the war had taken a great toll of Russian lives and materials. The government faced immense difficulties: victory against Germany was remote and seemingly unattainable. As a result of inefficient administration shortages and rationing were commonplace. To the middle-classes these difficulties seemed merely temporary and few foresaw revolt. The introduction of bread-rationing in Petrograd in March started a run on the bakeries, leading to a chronic shortage. This, to many workers, was the final degradation. Two hundred thousand workmen came out on strike, which soon brought about a general strike. Some strikers were shot and killed by troops and the following day Nicholas II dissolved the *Duma*.

In 1917, the Russian Army was very different from that which opened fire on the demonstrators in January 1905: they were now in their third winter of war, and the shortages meant long queues for little food. Although Russia had more than enough food for everybody, distribution was chaotically corrupt. Price inflation was rampant, but wages had hardly risen for three years. Not all soldiers were inclined to follow their orders to suppress the workers.

The Winter Palace, St. Petersburg.

Many sympathised with the strikers and, on the day following the dissolution of the *Duma*, the Guards regiments mutinied. The same day, February 28th/March 12th, *Isvestia* first appeared. By then, with large crowds roaming the street, and the army (supposedly fighting a war) in open revolt, and with parliament dissolved, it was clear that drastic and firm leadership was needed. Quite apart from these difficulties, the Tsar was deeply distressed by personal troubles: all of his five children were suffering from measles, and one daughter developed pneumonia. He decided to return to his family, but revolutionaries blocked the railway line. Although Prince Yussupoff (the Tsar's nephew by marriage) had masterminded the murder of Rasputin the previous December, popular feeling was running high against the Empress: she was German by birth, and rumour had it that she was secretly working for the Germans. That night, in the beleaguered train, the Tsar, acting on the advice of his generals, decided to abdicate in favour of his son. But as the Tsarevitch had congenital haemophilia, the Tsar's doctor said the boy's condition forbade such a course. The Tsar then abdicated in favour of his brother, Grand Duke Michael. However, Michael was in Petrograd, unlike the Tsar, and could witness events at first hand. The following day, Michael himself abdicated, and the 300-year reign of the Romanoff dynasty ceased to be.

That day the revolution was announced to the world King George V, on hearing the news, invited Nicholas to bring his family to exile in England. They were to go by train to Port Romanoff (appropriately enough) on the extreme Northern tip of Russia, where a British warship would meet them. But the plans were

Barricades in the streets of Petrograd during the 1917 revolution.

Tsarist police taken prisoner by the revolutionaries.

leaked and the Provisional Government ordered the Royal Family to be arrested.

Few could really grasp the implication of what was happening and Rachmaninoff tried, like many people, to go about his business as best he could. On the very day of the Tsar's abdication Rachmaninoff gave a recital in Moscow for the war-wounded, and a further army concert of Tchaikovsky's First Concerto under Koussevitsky led to Rachmaninoff offering his fee to the revolutionary effort.

The Provisional Government lacked firm leadership: later, Kerensky gained ground, but his ill-conceived offensive against the Germans was completely smashed. Coupled with the disintegration of the army, the street fighting and collapse of law and order, a feeling of anger and frustration quickly spread. Lenin, with other fellow-Bolsheviks, had returned from Switzerland, followed by Trotsky from the United States: their single-mindedness, following the lessons learned in the abortive 'July Days' insurgence, led to the October Revolution. The Winter Palace, the seat of the Provisional Government, was taken, and the same day the Soviet of People's Commissars was established. By November 2nd/15th, the Bolsheviks controlled Moscow, and on December 4th/17th, Lenin asked for an armistice with Germany during negotiations at Brest-Litovsk. The Russian war with Germany was drawing to an end.

Following the war charity concerts, Rachmaninoff took his family for the last time to Ivanovka but whereas in 1905

82

metropolitan events had little or no impact outside the cities, at this time all Russia was alert to the news. The situation was so uncertain that Rachmaninoff asked Siloti to use his influence in obtaining visas for himself and his family to leave Russia but, with the country still ostensibly on a war footing, this proved impossible. Rachmaninoff decided to leave Ivanovka and travel to the Caucasus where they spent a fitful summer. The Caucasian regional government disenthralled themselves from central government control and civil war broke out in the region. Rachmaninoff, very worried by the worsening situation and unable to leave Russia, decided to return to Moscow. His final charity recital was in July attended by Marietta Shaginian, who had just married, and who spoke with him for the last time. This also marked his final appearance with Nina Koshetz. He gave his last concerto date in Yalta in September, playing Liszt's E Flat Concerto. In October, at the time of the Bolshevik offensive, the Rachmaninoffs returned to their Moscow apartment. What is surprising is that, given his history of demanding peace and quiet in which to work, and living in the thick of revolutionary excitement, he began work on a long-shelved ambition: the revision of the First Piano Concerto.

The new version, a far-reaching re-composition, was completed in Moscow on November 10th/23rd, with the sounds of insurrection surrounding him. By then, Rachmaninoff and his family had been brought into the new regime: his Moscow district had been formed into a collective and he was obliged to play his part by attending meetings and joining the civil guard. He was resigned to his fate when, out of the blue, came an invitation to give concerts in Stockholm. This was the opportunity he wanted, so after accepting he left quickly for Petrograd to obtain visas for the family. As the Treaty of Brest-Litovsk was awaiting ratification, and Russia was no longer at war with Germany, the situation had eased. The visas were granted and he delightedly called Natalia with the news. Accompanied by the two girls she joined Rachmaninoff in Petrograd, where the family boarded the train for Finland.

The railway line did not cross the Russian-Finnish border, so they travelled through Finland to Sweden by sledge at night: at the Swedish border they took the train to Stockholm where, after having had their journey further interrupted by being moved into different compartments in another carriage, they arrived utterly exhausted. It was Christmas Eve.

8 Brave New World

Apart from their hand-luggage and two thousand roubles (five hundred being allowed for each member of the family), they possessed nothing. Ivanovka, which he owned and adored was seized: he had no idea when he would see the lilacs at the gate again. His mother and most other members of the family were still in Russia together with his music, his pianos, the orchestras, the Bolshoi, his friends and the workers on his estate, his horses, his pictures, his motor-car and his personal belongings. The things which reassure people who they are, and remind them where they belong, were all abandoned.

But they were safe: tens of thousands of refugees had left Russia during the previous months, many illegally, and a large number suffered in their flight. Compared to them the Rachmaninoffs were lucky. They left legally and it would not be long before he could give concerts: his previous trips abroad had made him friends and business associates. Rachmaninoff's foreign tours before the revolution now stood him in good stead. They had no money, but Rachmaninoff had ten concerts scheduled in Scandinavia: on the strength of these he was advanced money for living expenses, but Christmas in Stockholm was so miserable they moved to Copenhagen in January 1918 to join Nikolai von Struve. They rented a small flat which was very cold, but Rachmaninoff was able to devote himself to something like eight hours daily practice to be ready for the first Copenhagen concert on February 15th 1918, when he played his Second Concerto. A week later he gave a recital of his own compositions, and then returned to Stockholm for the concerts which had enabled them to leave Russia in the first place. In a series of concerto appearances he played his Second Concerto (adding the Third later) together with the Liszt and Tchaikovsky concertos, and with solo recitals largely of his own music he was able to see the rest of the season through.

The Rachmaninoff flight from Russia was public knowledge: during the summer of 1918 he received three offers from the United States. One was from the Cincinatti Symphony Orchestra and another from the Boston Symphony Orchestra. The third was to give a series of recitals. Both orchestras offered him the musical

Tsar Nicholas was held captive in his own palace at Tsarskoye Soloe before being taken with members of his family to Ekaterinburg where they were eventually murdered by Bolsheviks.

directorship, great compliments and great honours. In addition the offers were financially very attractive, but Rachmaninoff declined them all. His repertoire as conductor forbade the acceptance of such posts: his standards were that he could not take on these commitments with little or no preparation. More significantly Josef Hofmann warned him of the intrigue surrounding American orchestral management; in addition, months had passed since he had conducted regularly. The United States was still a strange land although he had many friends there. The previous year three main orchestras in America began illustrious recording careers. In January 1917 the New York Philharmonic under Josef Stransky made their first records for CBS; on October 1st the Boston Symphony under their German-born musical director Karl Muck

85

recorded the finale of Tchaikovsky's Fourth Symphony for the Victor Company, and on October 24th Leopold Stokowski and the Philadelphia Orchestra recorded Brahms's Hungarian Dance No 6, also for Victor.

The United States, of course, along with the other allies, was still at war with Germany. Early in 1918, anti-German feeling in America reached fever-pitch. Karl Muck was imprisoned as an alien in March. The Victor Company made no further records with the Boston Symphony Orchestra for over ten years, resuming on November 13th 1928, but for Muck it was the end of the line in America.

The news from Russia indicated that the revolution was not a temporary phenomenon: in July 1918 a series of assassinations of the Royal Family occurred. First, the Tsar, his wife and their five children were murdered at Ekaterinburg, followed six days later by Grand Duke Michael (the music-lover and friend of Rachmaninoff) and the other remaining Grand Dukes. Civil War had also broken out in a confused and chaotic manner. Cesar Cui, the last of Balakirev's 'Mighty Handful', died on March 24th aged 83 and Safonoff also died.

Some Russian musicians including Koussevitsky and his wife, Stravinsky and Prokofiev among others, went to Europe, and Paris in particular. But Rachmaninoff thought the United States would afford him a better opportunity so he decided to go to America to find out for himself. He was still short of money but a fellow-émigré loaned him enough for the fares for all the family. On November 1st 1918 they left Oslo in a small Norwegian boat, the 'Bergensfjord'. After a ten day crossing they arrived in New York

A few months before the 1917 revolution the Tsar took delivery of this unique motor car, specially adapted for winter driving. After his abdication the vehicle was used by Kerensky, leader of the provisional government, and later by Lenin.

Metropolitan theatre bill of 'Samson et Dalila', 11 November 1918 on the opening night in New York.

harbour. It was a Sunday and the city was in pandemonium. The Armistice had been signed that very day and the following day, as they awoke in their hotel, the cease-fire was being celebrated in suitable style. At the Metropolitan Opera House Enrico Caruso and Louise Homer were preparing for that evening's inauguration of the 1918-19 season, a new production of Saint-Saëns's *Samson et Dalila* conducted by Pierre Monteux. The 83-year-old composer sent his best wishes for the performance, which also included the Metropolitan debût of the French baritone, Robert Couzinou.

It was a day of rejoicing all over the world, but the United States to which the Rachmaninoffs had journeyed was a different country to that which Sergei had visited nine years before. Musically, the country was rich — New York boasted two magnificent symphony orchestras, the New York Philharmonic and the New York Symphony. Its opera house, as we have seen, attracted the greatest singers of the day. At the time of Mahler's directorship of the Philharmonic, Toscanini was conducting at the Met and recordings had also been made by the Victor company of parts of Metropolitan Opera productions. Outside New York City there were professional orchestras in Baltimore, Boston, Chicago, Cincinatti, Dallas,

87

Detroit, Houston, Minneapolis, Philadelphia, St Louis, San Francisco and Seattle, with extended seasons, and all of them were conducted by eminent European musicians. In the 1918-19 seasons orchestras were being founded in Cleveland and Los Angeles.

There was therefore no shortage of work for a popular artist, as Rachmaninoff soon discovered. As he arrived virtually penniless, he decided there would be little chance of devoting much time to composition. His music was known and, rare among contemporary composers, had reached the hearts as well as the minds of the music-loving public. Since 1912, when laws concerning international copyright were formulated, he was assured of a regular income and recordings of his works had already begun to appear. Mark Hambourg, born in Russia at Bogoutchar in Voronez in 1879, had made one of the first recordings of the C-sharp minor *Prelude* for 'His Master's Voice' early in 1916, and Dmitri Smirnoff, the Russian-born tenor, recorded a song and *Aleko*'s aria as early as November, 1911. It was Hambourg who had given possibly the first performance of any of the pieces from Opus 39 outside of Russia, when he played Nos 3 and 9 at an Aeolian Hall recital in London on December 1st, 1917.

Once the Armistice jubilations had died down news quickly spread that Rachmaninoff was in New York, and a stream of friends and well-wishers called to pay their respects. He had the good fortune to engage a young lady, Miss Dagmar Rybner, as his secretary to help with the enquiries which soon followed his arrival. As his English was not at that time particularly good, Miss Rybner proved invaluable. Josef Hofmann, who had recorded for Columbia the *Prelude* in C-sharp minor less than a month before on October 11th, arrived to offer help and advice, which was much appreciated. Hofmann had already alerted several agents. Fritz Kreisler also called, and their friendship developed leading to notable collaborations. Within a short while life for Rachmaninoff became hectic: offers of concerts poured in and his services were in demand from piano manufacturers and recording companies. He had corresponded during the summer with Charles Ellis in the matter of the Boston Symphony Orchestra proposals, and although Rachmaninoff had declined them he decided to let Ellis handle his business affairs and appointed him his manager and agent.

Apart from the natural bewilderment which always affects new visitors to New York, the Rachmaninoffs hardly had time to settle in before they fell victim to the Spanish 'flu epidemic, which claimed hundreds of thousands of lives the world over. Natalia was the only member of the family not to succumb. Although Rachmaninoff was still inexperienced in his new life in a strange country, he refused to be swayed by glamorous offers from firms to sponsor their products — but later he did allow himself to be used in this way. He preferred to make up his own mind in his own time and he chose a Steinway piano from the many that were offered him. An admirer loaned him the music room of her home free from the interruptions of hotel accommodation so that, whilst recovering

Caruso as Samson.

88

from 'flu, he practiced sufficiently to make his début as an American resident on December 8th 1918 in Providence, Rhode Island. Rachmaninoff's technique as a pianist attracted the admiration and envy of many musicians, but he did not have a large repertoire. Although it is not true that he had never played other composer's music in solo recitals before beginning his new career as a touring virtuoso, he had to work hard to build up his programmes. His superb training and astonishing memory again came to his aid, and with a secretary, a manager, a piano and much appreciated help from all quarters, Rachmaninoff quickly adapted to his new life. Indeed, he had little time for reflection, for such was his immediate success that in his first season, he made no fewer than thirty-six appearances including a recital at Boston on December 15th during which he premièred his transcription of 'The Star-Spangled Banner'. Other notable events were the first performances of the revised version of the First Concerto in New York with the Russian Symphony Orchestra under Modest Altschuler, repeated in Philadelphia under Stokowski, and a recital with Casals when they played Rachmaninoff's Cello Sonata. The Philadelphia performances marked Rachmaninoff and Stokowski's first post-war collaboration, and Rachmaninoff was particularly impressed with this orchestra and its already fabulous young conductor.

At the end of the season Rachmaninoff, needing rest from the family's adventures, made his first visit to the West Coast and rented a house at Paloalto, forty miles south of San Francisco, on the shores of the south-western part of San Francisco Bay thirteen miles north of San José. In this idyllic spot vaguely reminiscent of Lake Lucerne, where the Rachmaninoffs spent most of their honeymoon, they were able to unwind and relax. It was a restful and pleasant time: Rachmaninoff's first season had been so successful that offers for the next flooded in. In addition, Rachmaninoff learned that several old friends had followed him to the United States including his fellow-pupil from the Moscow Conservatory, Josef Lhévinne and his wife Rosa, and more importantly from a personal point of view, his cousin Alexander Siloti with his family. With these great musicians a large part of the legendary Russian school of pianists transferred to the United States. This emigration coincided with the endowment by Augustus D. Juilliard of a Musical Foundation named after him, including a music school in New York, at which both Lhévinnes — Josef and Rosa, who was herself a distinguished pupil of the Moscow Conservatoire — and later Siloti became professors, keeping alive this precious tradition.

It was curious, considering Rachmaninoff's eminence, that he had not made gramophone records. Thomas Edison, whose system of recording was possibly superior to his rivals on discs, approached Rachmaninoff with a view to making five double-sided records. Between April 18th-23rd 1919, Rachmaninoff made his recording début and his first sessions yielded the Chopin Waltz in A flat, Opus 42, and the Theme and Variations from Mozart's

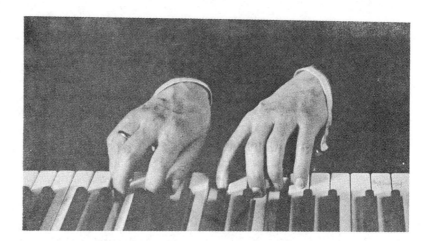

The composer's hands: a study from the early 1920s.

Sonata in A major K 331. The sessions were unhappy as the piano (an upright) was too far from the horns, and Edison commented the piano was not ideal for "this powerful player". The most important recording in this group was a three-sided version of Liszt's Second Hungarian Rhapsody, which lasts ten and a half minutes, containing a dumbfounding cadenza by Rachmaninoff (composed some time previously, but never committed to paper by Rachmaninoff, the version was first performed in Boston on January 10th 1919 at a charity concert). It is a pity Edison's inexperience in piano recording marred this highly significant recording for, although Rachmaninoff was not a pupil of Liszt, his cousin Siloti was (and had published a book in German in 1913 on Liszt) and Rachmaninoff's performance has special significance. He also made the first of his recordings of the *Prelude* in C-sharp minor and the *Polka de V.R.* at this time, in addition to his *Barcarolle* in G minor from Opus 10, a Scarlatti Sonata transcribed by Tausig and the 'other' A Flat Waltz by Chopin, Opus 64 No 3. Three separate takes of each side were made, but Edison disagreed with Rachmaninoff as to which was issued. In spite of the vicissitudes the records, which were released quickly, sold remarkably well, demonstrating that Rachmaninoff had strong commercial potential for a record company. His agreement with Edison was verbal, and Rachmaninoff felt their continuing relationship ought to be put on a more businesslike footing. Accordingly he asked for a contract, setting out several reasonable conditions, but the draft he received omitted them. This was not acceptable to Rachmaninoff and he returned it to Edison for amendment.

Charles Fuller Stoddard's Ampico Company also approached Rachmaninoff to make piano-rolls, and his first (apart from the abortive German pre-war recordings) issues were cut this at time. He made the *Polka de V.R.* and his transcription of *The Star-Spangled Banner* (which he never recorded on disc) in 1919, adding the G minor *Prelude* and one or two other trifles the following year. Rachmaninoff recorded for Ampico for ten years until 1929, but

90

with only six exceptions, from the thirty-five rolls he cut for Ampico, he duplicated his gramophone performances.

The three main systems were Ampico, Duo-Art and Welte-Mignon. Of these, by common consent the finest was Ampico, the most sensitive and sophisticated. Many artists, including Lhévinne, recorded for Ampico, but Alexander Siloti and Prokofiev, among others, recorded for Duo-art. Edison's description of Rachmaninoff's nervousness in recording—which never entirely left him—seems borne out by the Ampico rolls. The best of them—his later transcriptions of pieces by Kreisler, for example—are superb by any standards, but some are not completely convincing, in spite of Rachmaninoff's whole-hearted endorsement. This may be due to Rachmaninoff having been caught on an off-day, or imperfections in the restoration of the playing instruments, or Rachmaninoff not being entirely at ease with the system, but the later roll of the most important work he never recorded for disc, the Chopin Second *Scherzo*, is a strange performance, as reproduced, and it is difficult to believe that is what Rachmaninoff really meant. From time to time, attempts have been made to issue one or more of the Rachmaninoff piano-rolls, but it was not until March 1978 in London that the Decca Record Company re-recorded in the best possible circumstances every one of Rachmaninoff's Ampico recordings, for issue on three long-playing records, on their L'Oiseau-Lyre label. A remarkable demonstration of the Ampico system occurred on February 3rd 1920, when Leopold Godowsky, Mischa Levitski, Benno Moiseiwitsch, Leo Ornstein and Arthur Rubinstein appeared in a joint recital in New York during which, while curtains were drawn in front of the pianist, the Ampico recording of the same piece took over. No one could differentiate between the recording and the live performance, and the system was endorsed by the most distinguished musicians in the world. Rachmaninoff could not be present, for he was in Philadelphia to hear Leopold Stokowski give the first American performance of *The Bells*.

The 1919-20 season had begun on October 20th. Rachmaninoff's music rarely featured in the programmes apart from one or two works: his encores, however, almost exclusively comprised his short popular pieces, invariably ending with the C-sharp minor *Prelude*. Although he had sold the copyright to Gutheil (now taken over by Koussevitsky) almost thirty years before, he earned a substantial amount from the royalties of his own recordings of the piece. His concerto appearances were limited to his three concertos, but this was a more important season than the first had been. He had time to increase his repertoire as a recital pianist. He benefitted from his holiday in Paloalto although the whole family were very homesick for Russia.

The Victor Company had many distinguished artists on their books including Stokowski and the Philadelphia Orchestra, Fritz Kreisler and Pablo Casals. They were now anxious to obtain Rachmaninoff's services. Edison's tardiness in replying lost him

John McCormack with
Fritz Kreisler, 1924.

Rachmaninoff: on April 21st the composer signed a contract with Victor. A few weeks earlier, Kreisler and John McCormack, with Edwin Schneider at the piano, recorded Rachmaninoff's song "When Night Descends" with violin obbligato. Rachmaninoff was much taken by McCormack's beautiful personality, for after the season was over he arranged a Russian folk-song 'The Splinter' (*Luchinushka*) for McCormack on July 3rd. He harmonised another Russian song, 'Apple Tree, O Apple Tree' for a collection (edited by the American musicologist, Alfred J. Swan) published by Enoch and Company in 1921, entitled 'Songs from Many Lands'. This was his first meeting with Swan and a further friendship developed.

The news from Europe was sad: his friend Nikolai von Struve had been killed in Paris, falling down a lift shaft. Rachmaninoff heard the news at a summer residence he rented in the small country town of Goshen in New York State, about sixty-five miles north-west of New York City. This was another beautiful spot, calm and peaceful. It was soon possible for Rachmaninoff to make contact with relatives in Russia, and he was particularly pleased at being able through his bank to send money to them, including his mother. It seemed possible that he could visit Russia and he began making enquiries.

A notable musical event in the 1919-20 season was the founding of the Cleveland Orchestra with the Russian-born, American-trained, Nikolai Sokoloff as conductor. In this first season Sokoloff, who had a high regard for and a special sympathy with Rachmaninoff's music, performed the Second Symphony.[1] A particular favourite of this conductor, Sokoloff performed the work in nine of the next fourteen seasons, making the first-ever recording of the work for the Brunswick Company later in the 1920s.

Rachmaninoff's contract with Victor began to yield results. He undertook to record a minimum of twenty-five titles over five years with a guaranteed advance (recoverable against royalties) of $15,000 per annum, providing he remained an exclusive Victor artist, although he was free to make piano roll recordings. Victor were keen for Rachmaninoff to record some 'encores': the Edison recording of the C sharp minor *Prelude* had only just been released, so there was no point in a rival recording as sales would have been split and Victor were anxious to pursue their exclusive policy. Rachmaninoff's initial recordings for Victor in May 1920 comprised his two most popular *Preludes* (after the C-sharp minor), those in G minor and G major, together with Tchaikovsky's *Troika* from *The Months*. This was a favourite of Rachmaninoff's who recorded it again in 1928 but the recordings of the *Preludes* were the only ones he made. Victor's recording plans were growing: in December, 1920, Toscanini made his first recordings for the company, with the La Scala Orchestra of Milan (at that time on an American visit) at the Victor Studios in Camden, New Jersey. In

---

[1] Sokoloff had earlier conducted the Symphony in San Francisco, and later in Seattle, during his appointments with the orchestras of those cities.

An Ampico advertisement from the 1920s, showing Rachmaninoff's endorsement of this system

four days they recorded music by Mozart and Beethoven amongst other composers.

The success of Rachmaninoff's initial seasons convinced him that he would remain financially secure but his nature demanded a place in which to compose without distraction. He was also homesick: although he obtained the necessary documents, his plans to return to Russia fell through as he was now in hospital. For several years he was troubled by what he thought was eye-strain, which he believed was aggravated by composition. However, he had written nothing significant since leaving Russia and the condition had worsened: he agreed to an operation which unfortunately coincided with his proposed Russian visit. The operation was unsuccessful and only analgesics brought relief. It was several years before Rachmaninoff was finally cured.

His first Victor recordings were extraordinarily successful: the company, quick to capitalise on their find, recorded three more sides in October and November 1920: another Chopin Waltz (Op

93

34 No 3), Daquin's *Le Coucou*, and his first recording of Mendelssohn's 'Spinning Song' (which he remade in 1928). In January 1921 he recorded another Chopin Waltz, the E flat major Opus 18 and his own G-sharp minor *Prelude*, together with 'Dr Gradus ad Parnassum' from Debussy's *Children's Corner Suite* — an astute recording decision, for Rachmaninoff was preparing the suite for his next concert season, by which time Victor proposed to release the record to capitalise on the demand which would naturally follow. In April Rachmaninoff recorded another movement from the suite — the 'Golliwog's Cake-Walk', and two more Chopin Waltzes (one of which, the G flat major Opus 70 No 1, was not released until 1973). It seemed as though Victor intended Rachmaninoff to record all the Chopin waltzes, but in the event he only recorded nine of the fourteen.

In England, where Rachmaninoff's music was always well received, Sir Henry Wood mounted the first British performance of *The Bells*, which was postponed from the 1914 Sheffield Festival owing to the outbreak of war. This took place in Liverpool on March 15th, when Wood conducted the Liverpool Philharmonic Orchestra, with the Philharmonic Choir, and Doris Vane, Arthur Jordan and Norman Williams as soloists.

On the Jetty at Locust Point, New Jersey, the composer's summer home, 1922-3.

Before entering hospital Rachmaninoff decided to find a permanent New York home. He took an apartment at 33 Riverside Drive, overlooking the Hudson River. For the summer they tried a new location: a house in Locust Point, New Jersey, not far from the Victor Company's Camden studios, and Lakehurst, which was being developed as an airport principally for airships. At Locust Point the Rachmaninoffs and some fellow-émigrés established a Russian colony. It was a small consolation for his postponed Russian visit but it was memorable owing to visits from the Moscow Art Theatre, then touring the United States. Chaliapin also visited them, and the Moscow Art Theatre brought Rachmaninoff's *Aleko* to the USA. He took a driving test in New Jersey but failed, finding it difficult to cope with the English oral questions and the left-hand drive car (in Russia, his car had been right-hand drive): so he engaged a chauffeur. He chose a Russian for the post, and he also took on a Russian cook when their French chef gave notice. There were many applicants for the chauffeur's job. Fifty years later, there are still a surprising number of Russian-speaking cab drivers in New York. Another émigrée was Nina Koshetz who, with her husband and infant daughter, managed to leave Russia in 1920. She made her US debût with the Detroit Symphony Orchestra under Ossip Gabrilowitsch, the orchestra's conductor-pianist since 1918. Sokoloff engaged her in Cleveland and she soon established a new reputation in the United States. She and Rachmaninoff did not meet again until much later, but he gave recommendations to concert agencies and managers when she first arrived in America. Rachmaninoff was also able to correspond regularly with acquaintances in Russia, Morozov and Vilshau, so he remained in contact with his homeland.

For the new season, apart from adding the Debussy suite, Rachmaninoff planned a programme around various Ballades (he had earlier planned programmes with 'Studies' as the link). Now that Rachmaninoff's new life was firmly established in the United States, and his children had settled into their schooling, Rachmaninoff felt he had secured a stable enough base for further travels. A feature of this season was Rachmaninoff's first post-war English appearance followed by a visit to Dresden, where he was joined by his wife and daughters, so that they could all join the Satin family, who had also left Russia. During their stay in Dresden his sister-in-law Sophia recalled his daily habits, which included a short sleep in the early afternoon. In London he premièred four of the Opus 39 *Etudes-Tableaux* on May 20th. Earlier in the year he transcribed the minuet from Bizet's *L'Arlésienne*, which he premièred at Tulsa, Oklahoma on January 19th, prior to recording it for Victor on February 24th.

Rachmaninoff was deeply affected by the news of a great famine in Russia in the summer of 1921: the United States government made a huge gift of money and food but although humanitarian considerations were important the civil war, whereby White Russian forces continued attacks against the Bolshevik government, meant the anti-Bolsheviks might find their cause helped by this gesture. Rachmaninoff gave many concerts for Russian charities and famine relief and his generosity was much appreciated in Russia, where Vilshau had collaborated with the Russian composer Reinhold Glière to compose a cantata in honour of Rachmaninoff's fiftieth birthday, celebrated on April 2nd, 1923. The 1922-23 season was his busiest to date with seventy-one concerts in twenty

Rachmaninoff with his daughters Irina and Tatiana.

A further photographic study from the early 1920s.

weeks, extending from Canada to Cuba. Because of the travelling, he hired a private railway carriage fitted out as a travelling studio complete with piano. He soon experienced a universal inconvenience: the difficulty of getting a good night's sleep on a moving train, and he abandoned the sleeping compartment before the tour was over. In the light of this experience he restricted his engagements next season as he also wanted to give more European concerts.

Three days after Rachmaninoff's fiftieth birthday he was again in the Victor studios for more Chopin — the D flat major Waltz Opus 64 No 3 (the 'Minute' Waltz) and a Tchaikovsky Waltz from Opus 40. This was his second Victor recording of the Chopin, very different from the first, full of rubato and more of a 'creative' interpretation than the restrained character of the 1921 performance. Shortly afterwards Rachmaninoff should have travelled to Australia for a tour, but this was cancelled as he was physically exhausted by the season's demands. On May 1st he wrote to Vilshau in Russia:

". . . My dear Vladimir Robertovitch, I have received your letter with the many signatures as well as the Cantata. I was very much touched by the words as well as by the sound. Thank you all . . . I am not going to say more. I have finished my season and my hands are numb . . ."

Fully recovered but unable to resume composition, Rachmaninoff began the new season thankful his appearances were reduced by more than half. By the end of 1923 he had given only fifteen concerts and in his opening recital of the season, on November 13th in Scranton, Pennsylvania, he premièred a transcription of the Hopak from Mussorgsky's 'Sorochinsky Fair', although he had not written it down he recorded it for Ampico prior to this première. He completed the manuscript on New Year's Day, 1924. During a mid-season month's break, he recorded five sides of solo piano music on a single day (his most productive recording sessions up to that time), December 27th. The previous March he already recorded Moszkowski's 'La Jongleuse' and his own 'Polichinelle', so with these December sessions he had exceeded, in less than four years, the total requirement under the terms of his five-year contract with Victor — proof of his earning-power as an artist. The month's break also enabled him to prepare fully for his most important recording up to then: the second and third movements of his Second Concerto with Stokowski and the Philadelphia Orchestra. This was his first recording of the work (apart from selections from the Concerto on the lost piano rolls) and by choosing the second and third movements the Concerto was first recorded in the form in which it was actually first performed. It was common then for single movements from works to be recorded, but almost a year later, on the following December 22nd, the same artists added the first movement complete. Only one side of the Concerto's first movement was issued on 78rpm records: the second side was not released until 1973, in a commemorative album, and the third, which completed the first movement, was lost. The other movements were issued complete at the time.

Rachmaninoff's first recording of this Concerto is remarkably illuminating: swift, and entirely without the mawkishness often inflicted on it, several commentators have assumed that the tempi adopted were dictated by the playing time of the twelve-inch record sides. This is nonsense: the work was recorded with exactly the same tempi five years later, and the duration of the sides was significantly below the longest playing time then accommodated on a single side by Victor. Stokowski specifically rejected the assertion: Rachmaninoff's tempi he insisted (also confirmed by Ormandy) were chosen by Rachmaninoff, and not by the record company.

Several weeks after the January sessions Rachmaninoff and Stokowski were at Aeolian Hall, New York, where, on February 12th, a concert by Paul Whiteman's orchestra included the première of a work by George Gershwin (as Jacob Gershvine had become). Apart from Rachmaninoff and Stokowski, Sousa, Walter Damrosch, Leopold Godowsky, Jascha Heifetz, Fritz Kreisler, John McCormack, Mischa Elman and Igor Stravinsky all attended the premierè of Gershwin's *Rhapsody in Blue*, with George at the piano. Ferde Grofé, himself of Russian extraction, orchestrated the piece for Whiteman's orchestra, and the concert included another arrangement of Grofé: 'Russian Rose', based on the Volga Boat Song. After the *Rhapsody* the concert ended with Elgar's Pomp and Circumstance March No 1. Damrosch was so impressed by Gershwin's *Rhapsody* he arranged for Gershwin's Piano Concerto to be commissioned by the New York Symphony Orchestra. McCormack later recalled Rachmaninoff playing jazz for his own amusement, admiring several jazz pianists, and Rachmaninoff was taken by Grofé's arrangement of the C-sharp minor *Prelude*, which he heard the Whiteman Band play some years later.

At the end of the 1923-24 season Rachmaninoff gave a White House concert for President Coolidge and his wife, shortly after which he recorded Chopin's Third Scherzo. This was not issued as Victor already had a recording of the piece by Mischa Levitzki. It was first released in 1973 but Rachmaninoff certainly approved the take for release. More likely, the news from the Western Electric Company that a revolutionary system of recording had been invented — the electrical system, which outdated overnight all previous recordings — caused Victor to change their plans. Immediately after recording the Chopin Scherzo Rachmaninoff and his family left for Europe. They travelled first to Italy where they spent a relaxing time in Naples and Florence (free from illness this time!) and journeyed to Dresden. The elder daughter Irina, then twenty-one, graduated from Vassar College that summer and, during their stay in Dresden, she announced her betrothal to Prince Peter Volkonsky.

The couple were married in Dresden on September 23rd. The following day Rachmaninoff left for England where, starting on October 2nd, he had a three-week tour. The newly-weds spent the winter in Munich. During Rachmaninoff's British stay, the first English broadcast of his second *Trio* took place on October 12th, in Birmingham, by Nigel Dallaway, Frank Cantell and Arthur Kennedy — six weeks earlier Beatrice Eveline and Maurice Cole had broadcast the Cello Sonata for the first time.

Rachmaninoff returned to the United States in time for the first season's concert on November 14th in Boston. Although the concert season and recordings earned him a sizeable income, Rachmaninoff was uneasy that he had not composed anything important for years. While in Russia he began to note ideas for a Fourth Concerto, but the opportunity had not arisen for it to be completed. He needed a change of Concerto in his programmes but the Whiteman concert, among others, demonstrated that politics was not the only subject to have changed. He was now fifty-one, with his elder daughter married (and already expecting his first grand-child), and a younger generation of composers was springing up: Bartók, Hindemith, Stravinsky, Schoenberg, 'Les Six', all wrote in a new musical language.

Rachmaninoff rested from concert appearances for a while after December 1925, but first he completed the current season, during which he gave a second White House recital on January 16th. At the end of the season Rachmaninoff returned to the Victor studios recording another large Chopin work, the Ballade in A Flat Opus 47, but this also remained unreleased until 1973. Another work recorded at these sessions which was released was Beethoven's 32 Variations in C minor — or, rather, twenty-six of them, for nos 15-18 and 20-21 were omitted. These omissions were not dictated by the playing time of the 78rpm sides, even though the recording was issued on only two sides. Rachmaninoff's tempi for the Variations are remarkably swift, but he was not above editing other composer's music: pianists of his generation did similar things which would not be readily tolerated today. These were Rachmaninoff's first electrical recordings, and their improved sound quality is startling. Later in April the Victor company made the first electrical recording of a symphony orchestra: on April 29, Saint-Saëns's *Danse Macabre* was recorded by Leopold Stokowski and the Philadelphia Orchestra, inaugurating a new gramophone era. With the new recordings safely in the can Rachmaninoff left for Europe, travelling to Holland and then, for a complete rest, to Dresden, where he recuperated fully for five weeks before he was able to travel with his younger daughter Tatiana to Paris, where they met up with Natalia, Irina and Prince Volkonsky. They rented a chateau in the Seine et Oise Départment, south-west of Paris. No sooner was the family reunited than tragedy struck: Prince Volkonsky died very suddenly, just before the birth of his child. The baby was a girl, named Sophie, Rachmaninoff's first grand-child.

The sudden death of his son-in-law naturally caused Rachmaninoff to reorganise his life. Since Koussevitsky accepted the conductorship of the Boston Symphony Orchestra at the

Serge Koussevitzky (1874-1951)

At a reception in 1925 including Rachmaninoff, Stravinsky, Steinway, Kreisler, and Hofmann

Manuscript page of the Concerto No. 4 for Piano and Orchestra, 1926

beginning of the 1924 season, the 'Koussevitsky Edition' in Paris had lost its driving force. Rachmaninoff thought he could take up where Koussevitsky left off, and he founded a publishing house principally to publish works by émigré Russian composers. It was called 'Tair', after the first two letters of the christian names of his daughters, Tatiana and Irina, who ran the company. They published many works, including piano arrangements by Rachmaninoff which he later recorded for Victor and Ampico.

His decision (made before his son-in-law's death) to reduce the number of United States appearances each season to a maximum of twenty-five, made him dispose of his home on Riverside Drive. As a base for the six-week autumn tour of 1925, Rachmaninoff rented an apartment at 505 West End Avenue, on the Lower East Side. He attended Toscanini's much-delayed debût with the New York Philharmonic on January 14th 1926, a concert which included Resphigi's *Pines of Rome* in the presence of Resphigi, who conducted the work himself the following day in Philadelphia. Toscanini left for La Scala to prepare for the première of Puccini's last opera *Turandot*, which he conducted on April 25th. Stokowski prepared for an important American première, Sibelius's Seventh Symphony, with the Philadelphia Orchestra on April 3rd. Sibelius himself was composing his last masterpiece *Tapiola*, commissioned by Damrosch and the New York Symphony; its world première scheduled for December 26th, 1926.

While in New York Rachmaninoff began work on the long-postponed Fourth Concerto. He recorded more sides for Victor around Christmas, including his new transcriptions of Kreisler's *Liebesfreud* and Schubert's *Wohin?* which he premièred in Stamford, Connecticut on October 29th. Rachmaninoff persuaded Victor to allow him to make one of his most delightful recordings. He had met the Russian gypsy singer Nadezhda Plevitskaya some time before and had arranged a Russian folk-song, "Powder and Paint", for voice and piano. They recorded this arrangement together with some characterful additions to the vocal line by the singer, on February 22nd, and, although it was not published until 1973, the disc remained in Rachmaninoff's possession. It is a wonderful piece of gramophone history: few people could name the idiomatic and sly accompanist. The song exerts a hypnotic fascination in this delicious and deeply-moving performance. Hearing Rachmaninoff accompany this Russian folk-song, recorded thousands of miles from his homeland and performed with such aplomb, obvious affection and feeling, one readily understands the humanity and patriotism of this great artist. It is a side of Rachmaninoff's personality that was never again captured on record and one can only regret the missed recording opportunities of Rachmaninoff accompanying Chaliapin, for example, in the folk-songs they performed at parties until the small hours.

After leaving New York on April 20th, Sergei and Natalia travelled to Paris where they were reunited with their family before they all travelled to Dresden, where he completed the Fourth

With Nikolai Medtner in the 1930s.

Concerto. While writing the work he also completed a little-known work *Three Russian Folk-Songs*, for chorus and orchestra. The third is the "Powder and Paint" song he recorded the previous February: the haunting fascination of Madame Plevitskaya's voice inspired him and his months away from concert-giving enabled him to compose once more.

He sent the Fourth Concerto for copying and when the score was returned he realised the length of the piece. He wrote wittily to Medtner, to whom he dedicated the work, that it was so long it would have to be spread over three nights. Although Rachmaninoff had made changes to works in the past, after actual performances, it was the first time he cut a composition before it had been heard. It was doubtless this initial difficulty (also brought on by his years away from the composer's desk) in deciding the form in which his ideas should be expressed which accounts for the fractured nature of the Fourth Concerto, but it is a finer work than many people realise.

After his work on the scores Rachmaninoff holidayed in Cannes, returning to New York in November 1926: Leopold Stokowski (to whom he dedicated the *Three Russian Folk-Songs* Opus 41) and the Philadelphia Orchestra scheduled the premières of both works for March 18th 1927, but Rachmaninoff's own concert season commenced before that, in February.

The Fourth Concerto, despite gorgeous moments, seemed to many little more than an unsuccessful rehash of earlier works. Such a view is current fifty years later: it is a superficial one. Analysis of the slow movement of the Third Concerto reveals startling modernity (the first piano entry could be by Schoenberg), which reached a climax in the Opus 39 pieces, but the finale of the Fourth Concerto is utterly new. Few people appreciated the commanding newness of thought which entered Rachmaninoff's music here. The immense virtuosity of the finale is not dazzling passage-work to leave audiences gasping. It is hectic, action-packed music, unstoppable in its energy and power, unrivalled in its total use of the modern concert-grand piano, and orchestrated with a complete and profound mastery. In view of his later development, it is a pivotal work in Rachmaninoff's output. That one can speak of later development shows Rachmaninoff was certainly not finished at fifty-three. If the Fourth Concerto looks forward, the *Three Russian Folk-Songs* look back, towards a Russia dear to the composer. The work is brief, a mere fifteen minutes, and uses a strange chorus: no sopranos or tenors, only contraltos and basses, frequently in unison or octaves, singing simple songs with little decoration, accompanied by an orchestra commenting in a manner reminiscent of *The Bells*. The *Russian Folk-Songs* are as different from the *Night Vigil* as two choral works by a composer could possibly be, but the difference demonstrates the range of this composer, from the complex glittering polyphony of the liturgical work to the typically Russian Primitivism of the later piece.

In spite of difficulty with Stokowski over the tempo for the

100

"Powder and Paint" song, which Rachmaninoff wanted taken at a true *Allegro moderato*, it was this work which made the greater impression at the concert.

Rachmaninoff was disappointed by the lack of success of the new Concerto, for it meant a great deal to him. It was his first work for almost ten years; he had taken nine months off to compose it, and he revised it substantially before performance, but the critics judged it a failure. It was a tragedy the work was not better received for Rachmaninoff withdrew it for further revision, only to lapse into another period without composing which lasted five years.

On April 5th, Rachmaninoff was again in the recording studio for the usual sessions following the end of the season: he recorded eight sides but the music, apart from a few pieces by Chopin (including the second recording of the A Flat Waltz Opus 64 No 3 — which he first recorded for Edison in 1919) and two beautiful studies by Mendelssohn, is not worthy of much comment. It is clear from this repertoire that Victor were more interested in Rachmaninoff recording encores (for which there was a ready market) than in more substantial music, but this was soon to change. Rachmaninoff returned to his family in Europe at the end of a comparatively disappointing season, anxious to correct the 'faults' in the Fourth Concerto which he cut extensively, particularly the finale. The revisions occupied most of his free time during the summer. He enlisted the help of Julius Conus,[1] a composer and violinist (a brother of his old Conservatory colleague and fellow *Aleko* finalist, Lev Conus), whose violin Concerto in E minor was taken up by Heifetz. Julius Conus prepared a new set of parts from his corrected score, which was published by Tair in Paris in 1928.

If Victor were still only interested in recording Rachmaninoff in short pieces, the European companies were recording more significant music. The Beethoven centenary was celebrated in style by the English Columbia Company, who recorded several Beethoven symphonies under Felix Weingartner with the old Royal Philharmonic Orchestra. The 'Choral' was recorded in March, with Harold Williams as the bass soloist, and between June and October, Williams appeared in Sir Thomas Beecham's first recording of Handel's "Messiah". It was Beecham's Handel performances which helped secure his United States debût.

This happened on January 12th 1928, when he appeared with the New York Philharmonic. A sensational evening, it also saw the United States debût of the 23-year-old Vladimir Horowitz. His parents had taken Scriabin's advice when he heard the ten-year-old boy in Kiev, for Horowitz had already exhibited that grasp of cultural and artistic matters which Scriabin regarded as vital. He made his debût in Kiev in 1921, followed by a four-year series of Russian tours. In 1923 he played twenty-one concerts in Leningrad (the new Soviet name for Petrograd) in one season, becoming a noted chamber-music player. However, in 1925 he left Russia. His

[1] to whom Rachmaninoff's Opus 6 was dedicated.

101

recitals and first recordings — which included music by Rachmaninoff — in Germany, Italy and France created an enormous impression. Rachmaninoff heard about Horowitz from Fritz Kreisler, who saw him in Berlin and, as Horowitz's United States debût coincided with the start of his own season, he attended along with Josef Hofmann, Josef and Rosa Lhévinne and Benno Moiseiwitsch, the debût of Beecham and Horowitz. Beecham included four works by Handel and a Mozart symphony as well as music by Berlioz, while Horowitz played the Tchaikovsky First Concerto. Rachmaninoff met Horowitz the day before (January 11th) and wished him well, but the sensation which the concert caused leant an added urgency to Horowitz's second appearance. This was a concerto engagement under Damrosch with the other New York Orchestra, the New York Symphony, with whom he was engaged to play Rachmaninoff's Third Concerto on February 23rd. Damrosch had conducted the première with Rachmaninoff in 1909 and Rachmaninoff arranged to meet Horowitz at the Steinway Salon, to play through his Concerto. Once news got out that Horowitz and Rachmaninoff were to rehearse with Horowitz playing the solo part on one piano and Rachmaninoff the orchestral part on another, a crowd gathered outside Steinways, blocking the traffic. Horowitz recalls that Rachmaninoff said very little, merely making a few suggestions, but Abram Chasins said that Rachmaninoff "told me that he was completely astounded, that he listened open-mouthed as Horowitz pounced upon the fiendish piece with the fury and voraciousness of a tiger. 'He swallowed it whole', said Rachmaninoff."

The Horowitz debût impressed Rachmaninoff enormously, and the performance of his Third Concerto was especially memorable. Rachmaninoff had devised a new linked programme to complement those he had given in earlier years: a programme of 'Fantasy-Sonatas', including Beethoven's *Moonlight* and Litzt's *Dante*. In April he was again recording for Victor, or rather re-recording in the new electrical process, proving his continued popular success as an artist in spite of his comparative failure as a composer the previous season. The new recordings included his third, and definitive, version of the C-sharp minor *Prelude*. Eldridge Johnson's Victor Company was just one of many successful companies that blossomed in America during the 1920s and, after thirty years, Johnson decided to take his profit and leave. In 1927 he sold the Victor Company to a consortium of merchant bankers for £6 million, or around 20 million dollars. The bankers in turn began negotiations with the vast Radio Corporation of America, to whom they sold the Victor Company for a substantial profit in 1929. The Radio Corporation of America, or RCA as it came to be known, realised that in Rachmaninoff they had a big selling artist, and planned a series of more important recordings with him. In addition, the ties formed at the turn of the century with 'His Master's Voice' in Europe meant that the Victor Company's artists' recordings were as well-known in that continent as in the United

Vladimir Horowitz.

Sergei Rachmaninoff

NEW VICTOR RECORDS
ORTHOPHONIC RECORDING
FEBRUARY 1930

RACHMANINOFF AND KREISLER RECORD A BEETHOVEN SONATA

RACHMANINOFF

KREISLER

It is seldom that music-lovers in this country have the opportunity of hearing these two famous artists in a joint concert. Hence, this new Victor recording (Nos. 8163-8164) will be of peculiar interest. The G Major Sonata of Beethoven (Opus 30, No. 3) for piano and violin is in three movements. The first of these is lively. Violin and ... First

heard in beautifully blended ensemble. In the second movement the tempo is slower and the melody more warmly lyric. The exquisite tone of KREISLER's violin lends super-loveliness to this movement, even as the crystal clarity of RACHMANINOFF's notes. The final movement flashes a sparkling *allegro vivace*, smoothly mastered by the genius of these two titans, and brings this ... satisfactory close.

The announcement for the Rachmaninoff and Kreisler recording

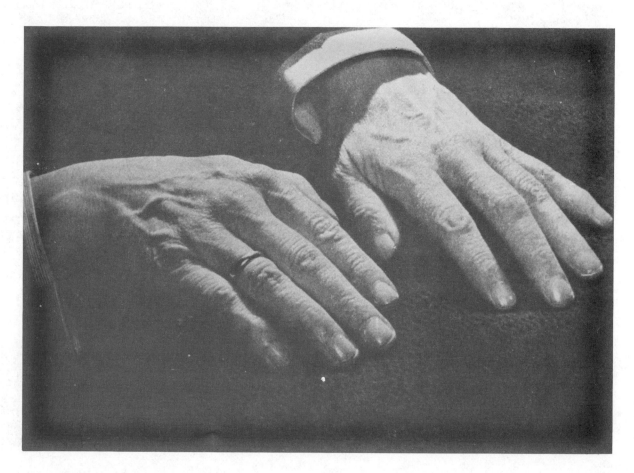

Rachmaninoff's hands

States, and the connection meant many artists were able to record for both companies in both continents.

Rachmaninoff had long wanted to work with Fritz Kreisler, and they recorded the Beethoven Violin Sonata in G major Opus 30 No 3 on March 22nd 1928. Together with Rachmaninoff's recording of the Beethoven Variations, these performances make one wish Victor or RCA had recorded more of Rachmaninoff in Beethoven. The sessions with Kreisler (Rachmaninoff's first chamber music recording) had gone so well they decided to record more sonatas, this time in Europe. A year or so before Kreisler had recorded, for the first time, the Beethoven Violin Concerto under Leo Blech in Berlin, and in this city Kreisler and Rachmaninoff (staying nearby in Dresden) recorded Greig's Third Violin Sonata on September 14/15th and, for the Schubert Centenary, the Schubert Grand Duo in A major on December 20/21st. These were regrettably the only collaborations between Rachmaninoff and Kreisler on record, but at the time they constituted a substantial recording project. The performances are suffused with a rapport that only comes from an intuitive partnership.

Curiously enough, early in 1928 Rachmaninoff completed for Ampico a substantial recording project which had been built up over several years, and which he never repeated for disc. This was the complete set of the *Morceaux de Fantasie,* Opus 3, which heard in sequence for the first time on the Decca 1978 re-recording is a remarkably impressive achievement, with few allowances having to be made for the slight variation in roll quality.

During his European stay while holidaying on the Northern French coast, Rachmaninoff took the opportunity of playing the revised version of the Fourth Concerto to Medtner, who was living close by, as were other friends. Together they formed another congenial colony of Russian expatriates, and in the autumn Rachmaninoff began his European tour with concerts in Copenhagen in October, followed by appearances in Scandinavia, Holland, Germany, Czechoslovakia, Austria, Hungary and France. The tour was immensely successful, and Rachmaninoff determined that future seasons would be similarly planned. The new year saw him in America for thirty-one concerts in the spring, at the end of which, in ten days, from April 10th-20th, he undertook a staggering recording project for the company which had now become RCA Victor: Schumann's *Carneval* Opus 9 complete; Rimsky-Korsakov's *Flight of the Bumble Bee* and Scriabin's Prelude in F sharp minor Opus 11 No 8; a new recording with Stokowski and the Philadelphia Orchestra of his Second Concerto, and finally his first appearance as conductor on record (and the first recording the Philadelphia Orchestra made with anyone other than Stokowski) — his symphonic poem *The Isle of The Dead*, and the orchestral version of the *Vocalise*.

This is an enormous amount of music to be recorded by one artist in a triple rôle within a few days, and a practical demonstration of the company's faith in Rachmaninoff as an artist. The future

103

Fritz Kreisler *Photo: RCA.*

looked bright indeed.

It was a time of great prosperity for the United States: the Rachmaninoff recordings in 1929 clearly show the huge investment available for recordings (RCA were also recording Toscanini and the New York Philharmonic,[1] and Stokowski and the Philadelphia Orchestra, among others, at the same time).

The summer of 1929 found Rachmaninoff in Europe at a rented villa called *Le Pavillon* in the village of Clairfontaine, not far from where they stayed in the summer of 1925 at the time of Prince Volkonsky's death. The new house, described by visitors as

[1] The New York Philharmonic and the New York Symphony orchestras merged in 1928, to form the 'Philharmonic-Symphony Orchestra of New York'

104

Two portraits of Feodor Chaliapin by his son: left 1928, right 1932.

'château-like', enabled Rachmaninoff and his family to re-create the kind of life they enjoyed at Ivanovka, away from the cares of the world. Alfred and Katherine Swan, whose description it was, left an evocative account of this idyllic scene:

. . . The whole arrangement was very much like that of an old Russian estate. The park of *Le Pavillon* adjoined the summer residence of the President of France. A small gate opened into the vast hunting-grounds: pine-woods with innumerable rabbits. Rachmaninoff loved to sit under the pine-trees and watch the games and pranks of the rabbits . . .

Among the house guests were the Chaliapins, whose son Fedya, a talented painter, persuaded the Rachmaninoff family to participate in home-movies. Rachmaninoff was able to relax completely at *Le Pavillon,* but he was saddened by the news of the death of his mother in Novgorod in September 1929. The news of her death came too late for him to attend the funeral, even if he had been able to obtain the necessary permits, as he was himself undergoing medical treatment. The facial pain from which he suffered was now correctly diagnosed and eventually cured by a Parisian dental surgeon, Kostritsky, a fellow Russian.

The pattern of the forthcoming concert season had already been established in previous years. It opened with five appearances in Holland commencing on October 19th, and a more extended British tour, with fifteen concerts, including two London recitals and a concerto appearance with Albert Coates playing the Fourth Concerto. This was repeated in Paris under Jascha Horenstein, but the work still failed to appeal to audiences. By the time of Rachmaninoff's visit to the United States at the beginning of 1930, the effects of the Wall Street Crash the previous October were beginning to make themselves felt. Rachmaninoff had lost money

105

following the stock market collapse but the larger corporations, such as RCA, were able to survive the losses even though it meant a drastic re-appraisal of their commitments. For Rachmaninoff, RCA had every reason to continue their association with him. His first appearances in 1930 included a Carnegie Hall recital on February 15th, in which the Chopin B flat minor Sonata drew from W. J. Henderson in the New York *Sun* the following:

... For one listener this interpretation of the B flat minor Sonata — in which even the Funeral March was played differently — closed itself with a magisterial *quod erat demonstrandum* which left no ground for argument. The logic of the thing was impervious; the plan was invulnerable; the proclamation was imperial. There was nothing left for us but to thank our stars that we had lived when Rachmaninoff did and heard him, out of the divine might of his genius, re-create a masterpiece. It was a day of genius understanding genius. One does not often get the opportunity to be present when such forces are at work. But one thing must not be forgotten: there was no iconoclast engaged: Chopin was still Chopin ...

This eulogy was not written by a critic to whom superlatives were commonplace: it shows that Rachmaninoff was at the height of his interpretive powers and explains why musical fulfilment was possible through his concert appearances. During the English tour towards the end of 1929, Rachmaninoff gave an interview to the *Musical Times* which was published in June 1930. This, together with Henderson's review a few months before, shows how his thinking had changed over the years:

... The older we get, the more we lose that divine self-confidence which is the treasure of youth, and the fewer are those moments when we believe that what we have done is good. We get lucrative contracts — more, in fact, than we can accept — but we are still longing for that inner satisfaction which is independent of outside success, and which we felt at the beginning of our career at the time of our troubles when success seemed far away.

Nowadays it very rarely happens to feel sincerely satisfied with myself, to feel that what I do is really a success. Such occasions stick in the memory for a long time — for nearly the rest of my life. I recollect the city where I felt this thrill of satisfaction last, and I remember all the details. I remember the concert hall, where everything seemed to me to be perfect that night — the lighting, the piano, the audience. Only on such nights do I feel happy and satisfied ...

Rachmaninoff with his grand-daughter Sophie Volkonsky on board the *Leviathan* in February 1929.

The Carnegie Hall concert in February was possibly one such occasion, for three days after the concert Rachmaninoff recorded the Sonata for RCA. He was obviously in top form, as the result is possibly his greatest recorded performance as a solo pianist. In addition, for each of the seven sides either the first or second takes were used. The set appeared unusually: four ten-inch 78 rpm records, with the E minor posthumous waltz as the fill-up. The Funeral March was obviously the focal point of the interpretation, for it was recorded out of sequence, the finale being recorded before the third movement. The most startling aspect of Rachmaninoff's interpretation is the change of dynamics at the reprise of the march, *fortissimo* instead of Chopin's *pianissimo*. The effect underlines the tragedy of the march, and other pianists have followed

106

Rachmaninoff's innovation, which was not a spur-of-the-moment whim but a deeply considered change.

While in the United States, Rachmaninoff missed the first English performance of the *Three Russian Folk-Songs* given by Sir Henry Wood in Liverpool on March 11th. The concert was broadcast by the recently-formed British Broadcasting Corporation (BBC) and the work was sung in English, translated by Kurt Schindler. Rachmaninoff returned to Europe the following month, sailing direct to France, where they stayed again at Clairfontaine. During this holiday, Rachmaninoff was approached by two people: his old friend from Dresden Oskar von Reisemann, and an Englishman Richard Holt, who wished to publish his memoirs. He collected some material and sent it to them, but Holt died in London before his work could proceed. Reisemann, however, invited Rachmaninoff and his wife to join him at his home by Lake Lucerne. The Rachmaninoffs were so taken by the beauty of the place that they decided to make it their home. Rachmaninoff bought land on the Vierwaldstätter See at Hertenstein, near Lucerne, and commissioned a reputable firm of local architects and builders to put up plans and build the residence.

In spite of Rachmaninoff's enthusiasm for the new villa to be built in Switzerland, in a closing paragraph in the *Musical Times* interview he revealed where his heart really lay:

"There is, however, a burden which age perhaps is laying on my shoulders. Heavier than any other, it was unknown to me in my youth. It is that I have no country. I had to leave the land where I was born, where I passed my youth, where I struggled and suffered all the sorrows of the young, and where I finally achieved success.

The whole world is open to me, and success awaits me everywhere. Only one place is closed to me, and that is my own country — Russia . . ."

Although Rachmaninoff meant that remark in a personal way, knowing from Vilshau and others that his latest works along with his earlier masterpieces were frequently performed in the U.S.S.R., within a few months of the interview was published even that link was closed.

9 The Hectic Thirties

Towards the end of 1930 the Indian philosopher Rabindranath Tagore visited the United States and, during a newspaper interview and in subsequent broadcasts, he spoke highly of the advances of the free education system which the Bolsheviks introduced into communist Russia. Tagore made the observation that a similar approach to India's educational problems might bring about a similar rise in literacy in the sub-continent.

Whilst Tagore offered no comments on the political system under which this education prospered, his remarks appeared at a time when anti-Russian feeling was running very high. After Lenin's death in 1924, a power-struggle ensued until Stalin emerged in December 1925 as the leader of a ruthless and severe regime. All traces of the old class-structure were eliminated, opposition was silenced, and Russia became economically self-sufficient. This meant a reign of terror against all dissidents and it was against this background that a group of Russian émigrés, stung by Tagore's apparent sympathy with Stalin's purges (although he had not supported such measures), invited Rachmaninoff to be co-signatory of a letter to the *New York Times*. It was published on January 15th, 1931, a scathing condemnation of the Stalinist regime. Rachmaninoff was never a political animal and, not wishing to offend his friends by refusing to sign the letter, he committed a serious error of judgement. It did not appear so at the time: the Stalinist regime well merited the criticism. But his action was based on a misunderstanding of Tagore's remarks and, although the USA had severed diplomatic relations with Russia years before, the letter was not unheeded.

Two months later the Russian-born conductor Albert Coates (who left the country in 1917 and became a naturalised British subject) conducted *The Bells* in Moscow at the Conservatory. The press rose to the challenge and Rachmaninoff, his music, Balmont, Poe, and Albert Coates were all condemned. Ten days later an edict called for a ban on all performances of Rachmaninoff's music in Russia. It was taken up, and his music disappeared from concert programmes.

However much Rachmaninoff became *persona non grata* in

Russia, in the West his music was as popular as ever even though the economic conditions led to a fall in concert attendances and record sales.[1] RCA considered dropping several of their artists, including Horowitz, whose services were quickly snapped up by EMI, the giant record company recently formed by the merger of "His Master's Voice" and Columbia. Following the Horowitz recording of Rachmaninoff's G minor *Prelude* the previous December, EMI now put together Horowitz and Albert Coates in June 1931 to make the first recording of Rachmaninoff's Third Concerto, with the London Symphony Orchestra. Although Horowitz recorded the work on two occasions later, in 1951 and 1978, the earliest performance clearly demonstrates his command of the Concerto. Horowitz's 1931 performance is still unequalled, for not even Rachmaninoff phrased the first movement's second subject with such pluperfect judgement and taste — although Rachmaninoff's own conception is quite different from that of Horowitz — causing Rachmaninoff to exclaim that Horowitz was 'the only player in the world of this piece.' Some years later in 1942, at a concert in Pasadena, California, Rachmaninoff made his one and only appearance on stage after hearing another's performance of his music, when he embraced Horowitz publicly following an irresistible performance of this Concerto.

Irresistible or not, Horowitz's two earlier recordings both contain cuts in the Concerto which have been made by others, including Rachmaninoff. Following the somewhat cool reception of the Third Concerto in 1909, Rachmaninoff felt the structure could be improved by cuts, especially in the finale, which uses material from earlier movements. At his meeting with Horowitz in January 1928 Rachmaninoff again suggested the cuts, with which Horowitz concurred, anxious not to upset the composer. Today, however, most people feel the cuts to be unnecessary in an age familiar with the gigantic symphonies of Mahler and Bruckner, and prefer the work to be played complete, which is how Horowitz played it in January 1978 for his third recording (apart from two bars in the first movement cadenza), which commemorated the fiftieth anniversary of his United States début. While Horowitz was in London for the recording with Albert Coates Rachmaninoff was also in Europe, where the two men met again, Rachmaninoff staying with his family at Clairfontaine. The circle of Russian friends was enhanced by a visit from Chaliapin, whose recording of the aria from *Aleko* made on November 11th 1929 in London, conducted by Lawrence Collingwood, had just been released by HMV. It is a deeply-moving performance, showing Chaliapin's genius as clearly as the recordings of Rachmaninoff and Horowitz show theirs.

It was a busy summer for Rachmaninoff, for he began work on a long-postponed revision, that of the Second Sonata Opus 36.

[1]In 1921, record sales in the USA topped 100,000,000 discs. In 1932 sales fell to less than 5,000,000.

Writing about this revision Rachmaninoff compared it to Chopin's Second Sonata which "lasts nineteen minutes — and it says everything". By comparison his own Sonata appeared long and superfluous. In keeping with his willingness to cut passages from a few works written during the 'Dresden' period, Rachmaninoff's revisions of the Sonata both lighten the texture and shorten the work, but even in its new form Rachmaninoff was never satisfied with it.

Another work which he treated with similar disdain, but which is in many ways the best of his extended works for solo piano, was the Variations on a Theme of Corelli Opus 42, completed on June 19th 1931. The work is dedicated to Fritz Kreisler who introduced Rachmaninoff to the theme, which is not in fact by Corelli. It is a traditional dance tune "La Folia", used by Corelli as the theme for a set of variations for violin. Rachmaninoff's twenty variations are grouped, as the earlier Chopin variations are, to form a large structure. They demand a fine pianist, but the piano writing is more linear than the heavily chordal textures of his earlier works. However much one is tempted to ascribe this rather increased astringency to a 'new' Rachmaninoff, clear presages of this style can be found in the remarkable Opus 39 *Etudes-Tableaux* and even more so in the finale of the Fourth Concerto. Apart from these unmistakable pointers, the tighter construction demonstrates that Rachmaninoff was not rehearsing the formulae of earlier decades. Regrettably the première which Rachmaninoff gave at the start of the new season (which began in the New World to enable him to travel to London for an important event in March 1932) was not a great success. This was in Montreal on October 12th. During the tour Rachmaninoff played the Variations many times: or rather selections from them. He sent a copy of the newly-published score to Medtner in December with a letter that shows he had lost none of his old tongue-in-cheek, self-deprecatory awareness:

. . . I've played them about fifteen times but of these performances only one was good. The others were sloppy. I can't play my own compositions; and it's so boring; not once have I played these all in one continuity. I was guided by the coughing of the audience. Whenever the coughing increased I would skip the next variation. Whenever there was no coughing I would play then in proper order. In one concert, I don't remember where — some small town — the coughing was so violent that I only played ten variations in all (out of twenty). My best record was set in New York where I played eighteen variations. However, I hope that you will play them all and won't cough . . .

Although three variations are marked by Rachmaninoff as optional, the work can only make its proper effect if all are played. Rachmaninoff's sensitivity was so great that he hardly ever gave this superb work its proper chance: no wonder its acceptance was lukewarm. And yet it was very possibly this lack of success (for this was the third work written after leaving Russia which had apparently failed) which discouraged him from writing any more music for solo piano. This is a tragedy for a Third Sonata, written in this style, would have been a truly remarkable work.

During this season, while the Respighi-orchestrated *Etudes-Tableaux* were being taken up, Rachmaninoff's concert with the Minneapolis Orchestra could have proved disastrous had it not been for the skill and musicianship of a young conductor, Eugene Ormandy. Ormandy went to the United States from Hungary in 1921 aged 22, and became one of the first conductors to gain practical experience in broadcasting. As he had been one of the youngest students ever to have been awarded the Gold Medal of the Buda-Pest Academy of Music his credentials were impeccable, and his ability to deal with problems under pressure made him the obvious choice to stand in for the chief conductor of the Minneapolis Symphony Orchestra, Henri Verbruggen, who was indisposed. The Rachmaninoff concert included the Second Concerto and the Second Symphony. Ormandy took over at short notice, and during the Concerto's performance, Rachmaninoff had a slip of memory. Ormandy's nimble thinking quickly saved the situation, which was much appreciated by Rachmaninoff. This, said Ormandy, "made us friends for life." Verbruggen's illness forced him to resign from the Orchestra, who offered Ormandy the position of music director.

At one of his last appearances in America in 1931, Rachmaninoff gave the first performance at the Juilliard School of a piece written many years before. He met his cousin Siloti there, and the work was the 'Oriental Sketch' written on November 4th/17th, 1917 (at the same time as two other short pieces for piano). This proved so popular that Rachmaninoff included it in subsequent recitals. He also premièred, on November 20th, two more transcriptions: Kreisler's *Liebeslied* and Rimsky-Korsakov's *Flight of the Bumble Bee*. Although the Rimsky-Korsakov piece had been recorded in April 1929 it was not released during Rachmaninoff's lifetime, but the Ampico roll of it was.

The composer with his daughter Tatiana.

During December 1931 Rachmaninoff returned to Europe for the second part of the season, made notable by a performance of the Fourth Concerto in Berlin under Bruno Walter. In London on March 10th, Rachmaninoff accepted the Gold Medal of the Royal Philharmonic Society after a concert in the Queen's Hall, where he played the Third Concerto under Sir Henry Wood. After the presentation, which was made by the Duchess of Atholl, the Rachmaninoffs travelled first to Paris to see their family, and then to Hertenstein, where the villa was well advanced. They decided to name it Senar after their initials, Serge and Natalia Rachmaninoff. During this summer their second daughter Tatiana, then 24, announced her engagement to Boris Conus, the son of Julius Conus, and a nephew of Rachmaninoff's class-mate of forty years earlier in Moscow. They married during the summer and settled in Paris.

Rachmaninoff repeated the format for the new season which he had adopted the year before, and returned to the United States to begin a very strenuous season of fifty concerts. America was still in the depth of depression.

It was not a happy season for Rachmaninoff: concert halls suffered like everything else, and there was little profit to be made. On January 23rd in San Antonio, Texas, he gave the first performance of his transcription of the Scherzo from Mendelssohn's *Midsummer Night's Dream*. But he was suffering from an attack of lumbago, so severe that at the recital he had to be helped to and from the piano. In order not to distract the audience by seeing him in pain, his entrance and exit were masked by curtains. It was the season which marked the fortieth anniversary of his debût as a pianist. His next birthday would be his sixtieth, and although he disliked a great fuss being made his friends in New York gave a reception for him on December 22nd, presenting him with a commemorative scroll and a laurel wreath. The season was over at the end of March on the eve of his birthday, after which he travelled back to Europe for further concerts. His return meant he missed the Toscanini Beethoven cycle in New York with the Philharmonic, which included an imposing Fifth Symphony on April 9th, and the 'Emperor' Concerto with Horowitz, and their meeting led to the pianist being introduced to Toscanini's daughter, Wanda. They fell in love, and were married in Milan the following December.

On his European return Rachmaninoff found the political scene rapidly deteriorating. The economic depression was particularly severe in Germany: after five general elections in little over a year, Adolf Hitler was elected Chancellor on January 30th. He lost no time: on February 27th the Reichstag building was burned down. The communists were blamed leading to massive pogroms and a demand from Hitler that absolute power be vested in him. On March 5th the Reichstag agreed, handing over to Hitler virtual dictatorship.

On May 5th in Paris a particularly happy occasion for Rachmaninoff was the concert at the Salle Pleyel honouring his sixtieth birthday and fortieth anniversary. Alfred Cortôt, the French pianist and conductor, spoke in his honour. Rachmaninoff's London recital on April 29th marked the English première of the Corelli Variations, but Rachmaninoff did not report on English coughing. The second half of the season's tours was more agreeable than the first, for Senar neared completion, and the Rachmaninoffs could see their daughters with their families once again. Apart from the occasional bout of lumbago and despite his persistent cigarette smoking, Rachmaninoff was in good health. The good wishes which had been offered him during the season did much to restore his normal demeanour, which was affected by the failures at the beginning of the season.

At Senar, Oscar von Riesemann's publishers sent proofs of his book to Rachmaninoff. The result was not what Rachmaninoff had expected: although he had talked freely with the author, von Riesemann made no notes during the conversations. Yet the book, as proposed, contained many passages in direct quotations as though Rachmaninoff had dictated every word. Some of the comments about fellow musicians, although one is inclined to believe they were probably correct in essence, were a little too near the mark for a person of Rachmaninoff's countenance. Although his artistic integrity was of the highest, and he was anxious to appear with the finest conductors and musicians, his innate good manners meant he would rather say nothing than to give offence when asked his opinion about fellow musicians. With von Riesemann it was a different matter, for he had known him for over twenty years, and was more free in his comments to him than to strangers. He demanded certain cuts and changes in the text all of which were complied with, and once the book was in a more acceptable state he supplied some manuscripts and wrote the foreword. Therefore the book as published was endorsed by Rachmaninoff, although he later stated in a letter that a lot of it was pure fiction. This makes von Riesemann's book somewhat unreliable as a result, but Rachmaninoff must take some of the blame. He had, after all, allowed the book to be published with his corrections, and by allowing his name to be associated with 'pure fiction' he was at fault. However, von Riesemann had suffered a heart attack before publication, so Rachmaninoff was unwilling to pursue the matter. We shall never know if his later comments were made to placate someone who had taken umbrage at a passage in the book. On balance, however, the twenty years' friendship and Rachmaninoff's endorsement of the book make one feel it might contain more truth than is supposed. During this summer, Rachmaninoff completed the score of movements transcribed from Bach's E major Violin Partita, and his own three-movement 'suite' taken from Bach's work, comprising the Prelude, Gavotte and Gigue, was finished on September 9th. Rachmaninoff found this an effective item with which to open programmes, which he did when giving the work its première in Harrisburg, Pennsylvania, the following November 9th. Another innovation was the acquisition of a large speed-boat, which became a favourite toy. He spent a lot of time chasing the pleasure steamers on Lake Lucerne, and he soon became an expert pilot. His skill averted what could have been a tragedy three years later.

The new season began with more concerts in the United States, including the première of the Bach 'Suite'. During his stay he heard the welcome news that President Roosevelt had resumed diplomatic relations with the U.S.S.R. Almost immediately the Russian ban on his music had been lifted, and Vilshau reported on successful performances of his latest works. The removal of the ban on Rachmaninoff's music was partly a result of President Roosevelt's diplomatic moves but Stalin himself began, early in 1934, to take a hand in artistic matters. Shostakovitch's opera, *Lady Macbeth of Mtsensk* had been premièred in Leningrad on January 22nd, but later was the subject of a bitter doctrinal attack. Wishing to nominate a model for young composers to follow, Rachmaninoff's recent *Three Russian Folk-Songs* was praised, show-ing that even composers of the old school were still inspired by the

Rachmaninoff with his friend Baron Nolde on Lake Lucerne.

113

The composer at his desk at Senar

folk-roots of Russian culture, rather more in line with Soviet think-ing than the modernism and sarcasm of Shostakovitch's opera. A few months later Rachmaninoff returned to Europe, expecting to move in to Villa Senar. Before the season ended he had concerts in London (on March 10th) and in Paris the following month, when at long last the new house was finished. When they took up residence in April, Rachmaninoff was delighted with the gift of a new grand piano from Steinways, already installed in the house as a surprise. The house and its surroundings were delightful, in a spot which has attracted many musicians.

After a minor operation in Paris in May, Rachmaninoff returned to Senar and, inspired by his new environment which he endeavoured to make as much like Ivanovka as possible, he commenced work on a new composition. Working in great secrecy the score was dated July 3rd-August 18th. It was his Opus 43, the *Rhapsody on a Theme of Paganini* for piano and orchestra. The première was fixed for Baltimore the following November, with the Philadelphia Orchestra under Stokowski. The new work was an instantaneous success with public, musicians and critics alike. A little over six weeks later, RCA made up for their tardiness in not recording Rachmaninoff for five years by recording the *Rhapsody* in Philadelphia with the original performers, on Christmas Eve. The performance, which is quite simply inimitable, went at a tremendous pace, for the published sides were all first takes. This was a particularly busy recording time for Stokowski and his orchestra for within the previous two months he had recorded for RCA Tchaikovsky's Fifth Symphony and Nutcracker Suite, Rimsky-Korsakov's *Scheherazade* (for the second time) and Dvorak's *New World* Symphony (for the third time in seven years!). This activity makes Rachmaninoff's absence from the

114

Bruno Walter, Thomas
Mann and Arturo
Toscanini

With his grandchildren
Sophie Volkonsky and
Alexander Conus on his
estate near Lake Lucerne,
c. 1936.

recording studios all the more inexplicable. The recording of the
Paganini Rhapsody as well as that of the Second Concerto of 1929
received the attention of the Japanese Victor engineers in 1977, and
their issue of the recordings is truly startling, enabling us to hear
many details which are obscured on all previous transfers and often
lost on recordings made many years later. Such is the excellence of
the original recordings that one hears the odd wrong note from
Rachmaninoff and vocal contributions to the performances either
from Rachmaninoff or Stokowski. The work abounds in the most
felicitous touches, from the opening (where the first variation pre-
cedes the theme) to the joke ending (the only part of Rachmaninoff's performance which could have been remade), and the
combination of the theme with the *Dies Irae* is another highly
characteristic touch.

Three days after recording the *Rhapsody* in Philadelphia
Rachmaninoff introduced it to New York, in Carnegie Hall under
Bruno Walter, where it caused a sensation. In the new year,
Rachmaninoff brought the *Rhapsody* to Europe, where in some
countries it was preceded by the release of the recording. In
England Rachmaninoff gave the British première in Manchester on
March 7th, with the Hallé Orchestra under Nikolai Malko. The
performance a fortnight later in London at a Royal Philharmonic
Society concert was conducted by Sir Thomas Beecham and was,
by all accounts, a brilliant success.

Although Rachmaninoff hardly spoke about his compositions,
even to close friends, and managed to evade the subject when it was
raised, he must have been very pleased at the success of the
Paganini Rhapsody. It also afforded him the practical relief of an
alternative concerto to offer, and proved he could still write music
which struck home to its audience, after a lapse of seventeen years

115

and a number of less-than-wholly successful works. It showed that his composing was far from finished, and that he was no longer wholly dependent on a kind of archetypal 'Russian' melody.

For Rachmaninoff the summers of 1934 and 1935 were particularly happy. He was surrounded by his daughters and his grandchildren of which he now had two, for Tatiana had given birth to a boy on March 8th 1933, named Alexander. Sophie was nine years old in 1935 and preceeding well with her piano lessons, studying with her aunt's sister-in-law, Olga Conus. Rachmaninoff had even set some of his grand-daughter's childish verses to music. In these happy and contented surroundings, Rachmaninoff began work on a large orchestral piece: the Third Symphony Opus 44.

In marked contrast to Rachmaninoff's new-found peace of mind, however, were the sinister developments in Europe.

The events of 1935 moved inexorably along a tragically-familiar route. The Saar region, taken over from Germany by the Versailles Treaty, elected to return to German rule on March 1st, and on the sixteenth of that month Hitler broke the Versailles Treaty by ordering conscription.

At that time Rachmaninoff was engaged on the second movement of the Third Symphony, having completed a draft of the first movement between June 18th and August 22nd. The second movement is dated August 26th-September 18th. The onset of the new season made Rachmaninoff postpone the composition of the third movement. With his wife he left for Paris on September 30th, before travelling on to the United States where the tour began on October 19th. The success of the *Paganini Rhapsody* and the work he had thus far completed on the Third Symphony found Rachmaninoff in bouyant mood, able to withstand the rigours of a particularly extended season. During the European half of the season, he travelled further East than before, with concerts in

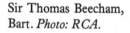

Sir Thomas Beecham, Bart. *Photo: RCA.*

116

Warsaw, Vienna, Budapest, Paris, Switzerland and England, where he made fourteen appearances. On December 23rd Rachmaninoff recorded his first solo piano sides for six years, but they were not important pieces: the Borodin Scherzo, the *Midsummer Night's Dream* Scherzo, and the Chopin A minor Mazurka Opus 68 No 2, the last of which (and most important musically) was not released. More recordings followed early in January: on the 3rd Rachmaninoff recorded Handel's *Harmonious Blacksmith* Variations (from the Fifth Harpsichord Suite) and his own *Serenade* in B flat, for the second time, replacing the earlier acoustic Victor recording of 1922. Shortly afterwards Rachmaninoff was in London for two Courtauld-Sargent concerts, at which he played the Third Concerto with the London Philharmonic Orchestra under Malcolm Sargent on March 30th and 31st. These were particularly fine performances, with Sargent showing a special affinity for Rachmaninoff's music. News had already reached Rachmaninoff of the death in Paris of Glazunov on March 21st at the age of 70, but a greater shock was in the sudden death of Respighi aged 56, on April 18th.

Rachmaninoff was in Paris in April for a performance of the *Rhapsody,* conducted by Alfred Cortôt. The French government at this time was gravely concerned by the occupation of the demilitarised Rhineland zone by Germany in flagrant breach of the Locarno pact. For Rachmaninoff, the beautiful villa Senar was a perfect retreat from the portentuous happenings in the rest of Europe. Here, in peace and seclusion, he could return to the unfinished Third Symphony: first, he revised the first movement between May 18th and June 1st and the finale followed — for it was in three movements — between June 6th and 30th. Leopold Stokowski and the Philadelphia Orchestra agreed to première the work the following November.

The composer with his wife in the 1930s.

In October Rachmaninoff was back in England. In London he played the *Rhapsody*, and later in Sheffield attended the long-delayed Yorkshire performance of *The Bells* for which he rewrote the choral parts of the scherzo at Senar before completing the Third Symphony. Both performances were conducted by Sir Henry Wood, who was interested to learn of the new Symphony. The soloists at the Sheffield performance were Isobel Baillie, Parry Jones, and Harold Williams, with the London Philharmonic Orchestra. Immediately after the highly successful performance, Rachmaninoff left for the United States, where he learned that Eugene Ormandy, after his five years at Minneapolis, had been appointed joint conductor — with Stokowski — of the Philadelphia Orchestra. After twenty-four years as conductor of the Philadelphia Orchestra, Stokowski had arrived at a point where his path, and that of the orchestra, were beginning to diverge.

On November 6th Stokowski conducted the world première of Rachmaninoff's Third Symphony at the Academy of Music in Philadelphia. In spite of a Philadelphia Orchestra tour with Rachmaninoff and Ormandy, when the work was heard many times

117

Leopold Stokowski
Photo: RCA.

in following months, the Symphony failed to catch on as the *Paganini Rhapsody* had done. The public and the critics felt the work looked back a little too far for comfort, but its qualities are too great to warrant early dismissal. The three-movement structure is a symphonic innovation for Rachmaninoff: but the central movement, beginning as the slow movement, contains the scherzo, before recapitulating the slow movement. Formally, this difficult inspiration is carried off with magisterial command: not since Elgar's First Symphony, which similarly unites movements, had a composer combined slow movement and scherzo — *and* a reprise of the slow movement — with such skill. The work shows true cyclical construction helped, as in the earlier symphonies, by the subtle use of a motto theme, combined almost 'as usual' with fleeting references to the *Dies Irae.* Rachmaninoff found himself yet again misunderstood by his contemporaries.

118

What was so new in the Third Symphony is a much greater economy of utterance: the proliferation of the first two symphonies, for example, is here replaced by a comparatively sparer style (apparent in the *Paganini Rhapsody*) which curiously enhances the emotional power of the work. The first movement, deeply tragic, is not morbid, but depicts a collapse so awesome in its inexorable tread that Mahler is often recalled. But unlike Mahler, Rachmaninoff's vision has the fateful objectivity of a Greek tragedy, finally overcome in the powerful finale.

Rachmaninoff must have known that in the Third Symphony he had written another masterpiece and its failure deeply affected him. But he had lived through a great deal since the failure of the First Symphony, and his virtuoso career brought the occasional concert where everything went right, which enabled him to recapture that rare spirit of delight, in spite of his frequent complaints about the peripatetic nature of his profession. Over twenty years before, in a conversation with Marietta Shaginian, he explained:

... Later he told me that every piece he played had a construction with a culminating 'point' (i.e., climax). And that he felt that one should measure and divide the whole mass of sounds so as to give depth and force in such gradation that this high point would flash, as, for instance, when the ribbon falls down at the end of a race, or when a glass breaks to pieces from a sudden blow. The culminating point could be ... at the end of the piece or in the middle; it could come as thunder or very quietly, but the interpreter should approach it with absolute calculation and exactness; otherwise the whole structure of the piece would fall apart ...

At each performance, therefore, Rachmaninoff strove to reveal the 'point', and yet this was always re-thought for each performance (even though the climax did not change). Abram Chasins recalled that his most vivid and striking recollection of Rachmaninoff was his manner of approaching each work, no matter how many times he had played it before, completely afresh as though it were a new composition. This sterling and profound musicianship was rare indeed. Therefore, there were compensations for the comparative failure of some of his works: the United States tour at the end of 1936 by Ormandy and the Philadelphians included *The Bells*, and in England, faithful friends such as Moiseiwitsch and Wood continued to demonstrate his unfailing hold over the public, for on December 13th in London, they performed both the Second Concerto and the *Rhapsody* in the same concert. On February 10th, 1937, Wood gave the first London performance of *The Bells*, using the revised Sheffield chorus parts, and the same soloists. This was a memorable concert, for in it Arthur Rubinstein played two concertos: Franck's *Symphonic Variations* and the John Ireland Piano Concerto.

The following month, March, saw Rachmaninoff back in Europe, first to London for some concerts and then to Paris and Senar for the summer relaxation. It was during this time at Senar that Fokine visited Rachmaninoff to discuss the production of a ballet based on the Paganini legend, which ascribed Paganini's virtuosity to a pact with the Devil. The music would be the *Paganini Rhapsody,* in which the *Dies Irae* made a highly appropriate connection. The ballet, in fact, was Rachmaninoff's own idea, as he outlined in a letter to Fokine on August 29th:

... About my *Rhapsody* I want to say that I shall be very happy if you will do something about it. Last night I was thinking about a possible subject, and here is what came into my head ... Why not resurrect the legend about Paganini, who, for perfection in his art and for a woman, sold his soul to an evil spirit? All the variations which have the theme of the *Dies Irae* represent the evil spirit ...

Rachmaninoff evidently had a very clear idea of the ballet's story, for he went on to link the variations to a definite plot. Towards the end of the letter he enquired of Fokine, "... You are not going to laugh at me, are you?" Fokine, far from laughing at Rachmaninoff, accepted his ideas with enthusiasm.

Rachmaninoff, along with countless other people, was deeply shocked to learn of the tragic death in hospital of George Gershwin on July 11th, 1937, at the age of thirty-eight.

RCA's continued unwillingness to record Rachmaninoff led EMI scheduling recording sessions at their Abbey Road studios for the composer to conduct the Third Symphony with the London Philharmonic Orchestra, on September 2nd-4th, to be followed by further sessions for the First Concerto a few weeks later. Rachmaninoff was somewhat uncertain about these sessions, as it was some time since he had conducted and the Symphony had still not been played in England. Furthermore the First Concerto needed practice, and Rachmaninoff wrote to Vilshau that he could "... not 'throw in', as they ask me, the recording of my concerto", even though EMI had scheduled the records for release during the winter, and despite the fact that he had included the Concerto in a London programme in April 1938. Finally the sessions were postponed, and never took place. On November 24th the London Philharmonic Orchestra under Walter Goehr recorded Rachmaninoff's Second Concerto with Moiseiwitsch for EMI, just six days after the orchestra under Beecham had given the Third Symphony for the first time in Britain.

While at Senar during the summer, Rachmaninoff attended an open-air concert conducted by Toscanini at Triebschen, and invited the Maestro to be guest of honour at a dinner-party at Senar a few days later. Among the twenty-two guests were Toscanini and his wife, his daughter and son-in-law (Mr and Mrs Horowitz), and the violinist Nathan Milstein and his wife.

In October Rachmaninoff travelled again to the United States for thirty-two concerts in little over two months, finishing on December 20th. During this month he learned of the formation of the NBC Symphony Orchestra for Toscanini, following the conductor's triumphant season in Salzburg and Bayreuth. The NBC Orchestra based in New York, although ostensibly formed for broadcasting and recording purposes, became a rival to the

Rachmaninoff and Toscanini

Rachmaninoff and Sir
Henry Wood in 1938.
(Sir Henry's Jubilee)

Philharmonic. In London, during February 1938, Egon Petri gave
an unforgettable performance of Rachmaninoff's Third Concerto
under Sir Adrian Boult. The European tour Rachmaninoff undertook early in 1938 brought him once more to London, where he
discussed plans for the Jubilee Concert to commemorate Sir Henry
Wood's fiftieth season as conductor. Rachmaninoff accepted the
flattering invitation to appear as the soloist in the concert — the
only foreign artist so honoured.

During this tour, he played Beethoven's First Concerto for the
first time, and was to have conducted the Third Symphony and *The
Bells* in Vienna in April, but Hitler's invasion of Austria on March
11th caused the concert to be cancelled. It was a mixed blessing:
Rachmaninoff returned to Paris, where he learned that Chaliapin
was seriously ill in hospital. Rachmaninoff visited him daily, until
Chaliapin's death on April 11th. He was greatly distressed at the
death of his friend for, among other things, he was a close link with
pre-revolutionary Russia.

121

Rachmaninoff slightly revised the Third Symphony before several successful performances in England by Sir Henry Wood. These included a broadcast on April 3rd by the BBC Symphony Orchestra in London, which Rachmaninoff attended. An all-Rachmaninoff Promenade Concert followed in August, including the Prelude to *The Miserly Knight*. Rachmaninoff was in London two months later for Sir Henry's Jubilee on October 5th: it was a glittering occasion, with the combined BBC Symphony, London Philharmonic and London Symphony Orchestras. In the first half, Rachmaninoff played his Second Concerto. The BBC wanted to broadcast the concert complete, but Rachmaninoff was wary of live transmissions and the performance was not relayed. However, he joined Lady Wood and other guests in her box for the second half, where he heard the première of Vaughan Williams's *Serenade to Music*, with sixteen solo singers. The conductor Felix Weingartner (in London for extensive recording sessions with the LPO) was also in the box, and recalled that Rachmaninoff was so moved by the Vaughan Williams work he sat at the back of the box, his eyes filled with tears. Rachmaninoff told Sir Henry he had never before been so moved by music. The reception accorded Sir Henry, Rachmaninoff, and the musicians gathered to pay homage, was tumultuous and at least Rachmaninoff knew that in England his music — including the Third Symphony — was greatly admired. The following day he left for the United States. His old friend Moiseiwitsch, who attended the jubilee concert, met Rachmaninoff at this time and, following the success of Moiseiwitsch's recording of the Second Concerto, EMI decided to issue a new recording of the *Paganini Rhapsody*. The popularity of Rachmaninoff's music meant there was a market for a cheaper version, and Moiseiwitsch recorded a stunning performance on December 5th, with the London Philharmonic Orchestra under Basil Cameron.

Following the American part of his tour Rachmaninoff returned to England early in 1939 for more concerts, including a Queen's Hall recital on March 11th of tremendous stature and authority. As it turned out, this was his last appearance in England. He was back in Senar in April, and as a result of an accident was unfortunately unable to visit London to attend the première of Fokine's ballet *Paganini*. Rachmaninoff had slipped and fallen heavily at home, and was shaken and lame for several weeks. The première at Covent Garden on June 30th 1939 was a tremendous success. Antal Dorati conducted and Eric Harrison was the solo pianist. By August, Rachmaninoff recovered sufficiently to appear at the Lucerne Festival where, on August 11th, he played Beethoven's C major concerto and the *Rhapsody*, with Ansermet conducting. A mystery surrounds this concert, which proved to be Rachmaninoff's last public engagement in Europe. It was scheduled to be broadcast and, despite Rachmaninoff's refusal to grant permission, it is possible that a transmission was actually made. Two days later, Rachmaninoff and his wife left for Paris.

It was obvious to everyone in Europe that war was inevitable. In 1938 Hitler's annexation of the Sudetenland went unchallenged by France and Britain at a series of meetings in Munich. A 'Peace Declaration' between England and Germany was brought back by the British Prime Minister, Neville Chamberlain. The partition of Czechoslovakia followed: on March 14th 1939, the Czechoslovak Republic was dissolved and the following day German troops began to occupy Bohemia and Moravia. It was clear that Hitler next had designs on Poland. As Britain and France both had treaties with Poland, German agression would inevitably trigger off another war.

In August 1939, against this background, Rachmaninoff decided to leave Europe for America, taking Irina and her daughter, but leaving Tatiana with her husband, Boris, and their six-year-old son, Alexander, in Paris. He never saw them again.

Rachmaninoff and his family sailed from Cherbourg on August 23rd for New York, the day before a ten-year non-agression treaty was signed in Moscow between the Soviet Union and Germany. A few days after Rachmaninoff arrived in America, Hitler used alleged border incidents as his justification to declare war on Poland. Two days later on September 3rd, their joint ultimatum having expired, Britain and France declared war on Germany.

10 Finale

With Sophie
Volkonsky, 1939.

The *Dies Irae* plainchant theme had always fascinated Rachmaninoff: it appears in all three of his symphonies, many solo piano works, *The Isle of the Dead* and the *Paganini Rhapsody*. In some ways, the success of the *Rhapsody* is all the more remarkable when one considers how the themes on which it is based had already been used. The Paganini theme had been chosen by earlier composers as a basis for variations,[1] and the *Dies Irae* theme formed the basis, among others, for Liszt's greatest work for piano and orchestra — the *Totentanz*, a set of variations on the old theme. Rachmaninoff admired Liszt's *Totentanz* greatly, and when considering a new concerto to add to his repertoire, he chose it to open his new season in the United States. It was a hectic season, but the 66-year-old took it in his stride. The highlight was the 'Rachmaninoff Cycle' which the Philadelphia Orchestra gave under Ormandy, with Rachmaninoff participating, to celebrate the thirtieth anniversary of his American debût. It formed a spectrum of his greatest orchestral music: the first three concertos and *Paganini Rhapsody* all with the composer as soloist, and with Ormandy conducting *The Isle of the Dead* and the Second Symphony. The final concert was conducted by Rachmaninoff himself: the Third Symphony and *The Bells*.

This was too good for RCA to miss: here was a golden opportunity to capture the composer in two of the unrecorded concertos and the Symphony. On December 4th Charles O'Connell, then head of the Red Seal Classical Division of RCA, supervised the sessions which produced the First and Third Concertos. Both works were recorded in a single day, but Rachmaninoff and the orchestra remade several passages a few months later. Although Rachmaninoff made many recordings he was easily disturbed by studio distractions unconnected with music, including the warning buzzer from the recording director, or the starting light which followed. It made him so nervous that at one point he slammed his hands on the keyboard and said he could not play in such conditions. Ormandy and O'Connell between

[1] And later composers, including Boris Blacher, Lutoslawski and Andrew Lloyd Webber

124

Eugene Ormandy *Photo: RCA*.

In rehearsal with Ormandy and the Philadelphia Orchestra, 1939.

them worked out a secret warning system whereby the red light was placed on Ormandy's right-hand side where Rachmaninoff could not see it, and three light signals replaced the buzzer. After that, one light gave the artists the signal to start playing. From then on, everything went well and Rachmaninoff's composure was restored. A week later, Rachmaninoff conducted the orchestra in a recording of the Third Symphony — a performance shows how much was lost when Rachmaninoff withdrew from conducting. Here is no 'composer-conductor' but a real conductor, whose control and direction of the orchestra place him among the great. Recorded the day following the final concert in the cycle, it is a tragedy Rachmaninoff did not also record *The Bells*, but the recording of the Symphony is so remarkable that Rachmaninoff's interpretation is annotated in the published score. The composer made a tiny cut of two bars in the first movement, and altered the metrical shape of the second subject. Conductors should not be so slavish as to copy these changes parrot-fashion: they should be guided by Rachmaninoff's emphasis, but it is a pity his example is often ignored. It is not true, as the score claims, that Rachmaninoff was present when Eugene Ormandy and the Philadelphia Orchestra first recorded the Symphony for CBS: Rachmaninoff had been dead for over ten years when that recording was made.

Apart from the concern over the progress of the war in Europe, this was a happy time for Rachmaninoff. The great series of recordings had gone well and the 'Rachmaninoff Cycle' had been highly successful. During the season which, on February 24th 1940, included remaking parts of the first movement and the whole of the finale of the First Concerto, and parts of the second movement and finale of the Third, Rachmaninoff also undertook the revision of several of the shorter early pieces: the second of the *Moments Musicaux* Opus 16 (on February 5th); the *Mélodie* in E and the *Serenade* in B flat major, both from Opus 3 (February 26th), and on March 3rd, the *Humoresque* in G major Opus 10 No 5. On

125

March 18th, Rachmaninoff was back in the recording studios, as a solo pianist for the first time in over four years, to record the revised *Moment Musical*, four Preludes, two of the Opus 33 *Etudes-Tableaux*, as well as *Daisies* and the *Oriental Sketch*. Three weeks later, he recorded the *Humoresque* and the *Mélodie*.

The most remarkable of the 1939-40 recordings is that of the Third Concerto. It is unique, and totally unlike most performances one hears. It is ceaseless in its energy, constantly thrusting forward with an irresistible drive and purpose. Rachmaninoff treats the immense technical difficulties of the solo part almost with contempt in his fiery and eruptive reading. Not that it lacks sensitivity: far from it, for Rachmaninoff's famous tone and flawless phrasing are there. The power, authority and tingling vitality of his performance constitute a master-class on how to play the work. What is more difficult to accept are the cuts. The finale has been fair game for almost every pianist since Rachmaninoff to cut at will, but the other movements are subjected to small, but important, cuts. Later generations accept this concerto complete; its unity and structure are appreciated more than when Rachmaninoff was alive. But Rachmaninoff himself insisted on making these excisions to tighten up the structure. This was much to RCA's annoyance, for it meant an odd side; without cuts the music could easily have been accommodated in the playing time of the remaining side.

At the end of the season Rachmaninoff rented a summer home at Orchard Point, near Huntingdon on Long Island, New York. Horowitz had recorded Brahms's Second Piano Concerto with his father-in-law Toscanini for RCA on May 9th, and visited Rachmaninoff several times during the summer to discuss Rachmaninoff's Second Sonata. Horowitz possessed both the original edition and the revised version, but felt the work was unsatisfactory in either form. Rachmaninoff agreed, and left it to Horowitz to prepare a new edition for his own use. But it was not until 1968, at Carnegie Hall, and appropriately, at the Academy of Music in Philadelphia, that Horowitz recorded his own version.

In the new surroundings Rachmaninoff again turned to composition. Between September 22nd and October 29th he completed a large-scale orchestral work: the Symphonic Dances Opus 45 which, in gratitude, he dedicated to Eugene Ormandy and the Philadelphia Orchestra, who immediately accepted the work for performance early in 1941. He already drafted the work for two pianos before the orchestral score, and in this two-piano form it is occasionally heard when it forms a fitting climax to Rachmaninoff's four large-scale works for two pianos. Although Rachmaninoff missed the performances of the *Paganini* ballet the previous year in London, Fokine was then living close by in New York and Rachmaninoff entertained hopes for a choreographic treatment of the new work. The Symphonic Dances was the only work Rachmaninoff wrote completely in the United States, but he had to hurry to finish the orchestration as the 1940-41 season began before

Sergei Rachmaninoff in 1939

Rachmaninoff and Ormandy during rehearsal in 1939

Franklin D. Roosevelt (1882-1945)

the score was finished. In August, he wrote to Eugene Ormandy:

... Last week I finished a new symphonic piece, which I naturally want to give first to you and your orchestra. It is called 'Fantastic Dances'. I shall now begin the orchestration. Unfortunately my concert tour begins on October 14th. I have a great deal of practice to do and I don't know whether I shall be able to finish the orchestration before November.

I should be very glad if, upon your return, you would drop over to our place. I should like to play the piece for you. We are staying at the Honeyman Estate, Huntingdon, Long Island, and only forty miles from New York, so that you can easily reach us ...

Ormandy, delighted at the news, met Rachmaninoff and invited him to the rehearsals, during which he addressed the orchestra:

... When I was a young man, I idolised Chaliapin. He was my ideal, and when I thought of composition I thought of song and Chaliapin. Now he is gone. Today, when I think of composing, my thoughts turn to you, the greatest orchestra in the world. For that reason I dedicate this, my newest composition, to the members of the Philadelphia Orchestra and to your conductor, Eugene Ormandy ...

The orchestra under Ormandy gave the first performance on January 3rd, 1941. The reception, as for the Third Symphony, was lukewarm. For the critics it was all too easy: they thought they had heard it all before. They had not: this last work of Rachmaninoff's is a new and vibrant voice in his music, expressed in a truly symphonic manner as almost to deserve the title of Fourth Symphony. In this work, the *Dies Irae* is again present, but in the coda, marked 'Alleluia', the *Dies Irae* is swirled into silence by the virile and invigorating resolution: D minor, the ultimate tonality for this composer, triumphs over all in the hectic, tumultuous and life-asserting closing pages. The orchestra is large and the work contains passing influences of big band jazz. The music swaggers, supreme in its self-confidence and burning with a fierce inner light. This is manifestly *not* music by a tired composer who had written himself out: to see the effect this exhilarating music has on audiences decades after it was written, is to witness an essential truth of this great musician's work. This music is not a reflection of a bygone age, fashionably nostalgic, but an indestructible and inspiring musical statement.

Shortly after the première, President Roosevelt was inaugurated for an unprecedented third term. Rachmaninoff prepared for more concerts, repeating the dual-symphonic programme of the Third Symphony and *The Bells* in Chicago early in 1941. The Philadelphia Rachmaninoff Cycle and the Symphonic Dances première, together with the release of the recordings, had focused attention again on the composer who, at 68, was becoming a legend. The magazine *The Etude* interviewed him in 1941, and he gave a clear insight into his attitude towards composition:

... In my own compositions, no conscious effort has been made to be original, or Romantic or Nationalistic, or anything else. I write down on paper the music I hear within me, as naturally as possible. I am a Russian composer, and the land of my birth has influenced my temperament and outlook. My music is the product of

The composer with Walt Disney and Vladimir Horowitz at the Disney Studios, Hollywood, in 1942.

the temperament, and so it is Russian music; I never consciously attempt to write Russian music, or any other kind of music. What I try to do, when writing down my music, is to make it say simply and directly that which is in my heart when I am composing . . .

While Rachmaninoff spoke eloquently of Chaliapin when addressing the Philadelphia Orchestra during the rehearsals for the Symphonic Dances, Nina Koshetz, the dedicatee of the Opus 38 Songs and an incomparable interpreter of Rachmaninoff's music, was still only forty-six and in good voice. The American music-publishing firm of G. Schirmer approached her in 1940 to record an album of Russian songs, in which Rachmaninoff's songs would feature prominently. Although Rachmaninoff and Koshetz had not seen each other since 1917, she had pursued a somewhat fitful career, which never quite fulfilled her early promise, since she left Russia in 1920. Madame Koshetz agreed, and signed her contract with Schirmer's on March 3rd 1941. The accompanist for the album was Celius Dougherty, who was no Rachmaninoff but the vocal performances are incomparable, especially the one song from Opus 38, 'Daisies'.

The war in Europe spread rapidly. Hitler invaded Russia on June 22nd, and Rachmaninoff, deeply concerned that Russia was again at war, decided to devote the proceeds from most of his concerts during the forthcoming season to the Red Army.

In August he made another transcription, this time of Tchaikovsky's *'Lullaby'* (Opus 16 No 1), and premièred it at Syracuse, New York on October 14th. In the event this was Rachmaninoff's last work as a composer: an appropriate transcription, of music by Tchaikovsky, but an incredible coincidence. Fifty-five years earlier, in another country, another continent, another culture, another century, the 13-year-old Sergei Rachmaninoff began his career as a composer with a Tchaikovsky transcription, the *'Manfred'* Symphony for piano duet.

The summer also saw the final revisions of the unlucky Fourth Concerto and, three days after the Syracuse recital, Rachmaninoff gave the première of the final version of the Concerto in Philadelphia with Ormandy conducting. He added a new concerto to his repertoire, the Schumann, which he played with his Fourth Concerto. RCA decided to record the Fourth Concerto in December, but on the seventh of that month the Japanese attacked Pearl Harbor. The American losses were considerable: over 3,000 men were killed or reported missing, and over 1,000 injured. The following day President Roosevelt announced that the United States had declared war against Japan. Germany and Italy declared war on the United States on December 11th. Arthur Rubinstein was soloist with the New York Philharmonic at Carnegie Hall when news came through of the Japanese attack. It was a Sunday afternoon concert, with Artur Rodzinski conducting, and Rubinstein spontaneously joined with the orchestra in playing 'The Star-Spangled Banner'. On December 20th Rachmaninoff and

Photo: RCA.

129

Ormandy recorded the Fourth Concerto with the Philadelphia Orchestra but, unfortunately, not the Schumann. These sessions meant that Rachmaninoff had now recorded all his works for piano and orchestra. After Christmas, Rachmaninoff's engagements continued with more recording sessions: on February 26th/27th he recorded his 'Suite' from the Bach Partita together with other transcriptions by Liszt and Tausig, as well as a second recording of the Kreisler *Liebesfreud* arrangement, and the Tchaikovsky *'Lullaby'* which was not released until 1973. Toscanini and the New York Philharmonic gave a series of Beethoven concerts as part of the orchestra's centenary celebrations. Rachmaninoff attended a Toscanini rehearsal for one of the concerts, and the maestro sought his advice over a particularly tricky passage for strings. Three months later, on July 19th, Toscanini conducted the western première of Shostakovitch's 'Leningrad' Symphony (No 7), composed during the German seige of that city the previous winter.

Rachmaninoff spent the summer on the West Coast, renting a house in Beverly Hills, Los Angeles. Not far away lived Vladimir and Wanda Horowitz and the two great pianists met occasionally to play Rachmaninoff's two-piano music, particularly the suites, and discussed plans to give a public recital together, once the 1943 season was over. Regrettably, RCA turned down the suggestion to record the suites with Rachmaninoff and Horowitz, so another priceless opportunity was lost. Some years before Rachmaninoff and his wife Natalia were recorded on a disc-cutting machine at Alexander Greiner's home. This recording of the *Polka Italienne* has survived, but it is technically crude. Rachmaninoff was much attracted by the Russian colony at the Hollywood film studios: composers, actors, film directors and the like were welcome company, and the Rachmaninoffs met up again with Nina Koshetz and her family (she had remarried) who were also in Los Angeles. They frequented each other's homes, and Abram Chasins recalled that hearing Koshetz and Rachmaninoff perform almost all the songs was a priceless and unforgettable experience. Once again, a unique recording opportunity passed by. Rachmaninoff decided to make his permanent residence in Beverly Hills, and to buy a house on Elm Drive.

As he was approaching his seventieth birthday in April 1943, he decided his next season would be his last, and that he would retire from public performances when it was over. His beautiful Beverly Hills home possessed a superb garden: here he would tend his flowers. First he gave a number of concerts (including a Hollywood Bowl appearance) for war charities. The season began on October 12th in Detroit, but he had been suffering from lumbago and tiredness: a six-week break was included in the tour so he could rest. In New York in December he played the *Rhapsody* with the Philharmonic under Dmitri Mitropoulos, who conducted the Symphonic Dances in the same concert. Only Rachmaninoff, in the audience, could have known of two important self-quotations in

Photo: RCA.

this work: towards the end of the first dance Rachmaninoff quotes the motto theme from his First Symphony, the score of which was still unknown and, in the 'Alleluia' section, from the *Night Vigil*. Following the concert a party was held to celebrate Rachmaninoff's fiftieth anniversary as a concert artist. The tour resumed in February 1943, but he still complained of fatigue and pains and a persistent cough, aggravated by his smoking. After several recitals, he played the Beethoven Concerto and his *Rhapsody* twice in Chicago. After the second concert his pains increased, but against doctor's orders he continued with engagements in Louisville on February 15th and in Knoxville, Tennessee, on the 17th. Rachmaninoff was particularly anxious to play in Knoxville as he had been obliged to cancel a recital there some years before. While on the train to Florida he became very ill and, following doctor's advice this time, the remaining concerts were cancelled. He travelled south to New Orleans for the warmer air, where it was hoped his condition might improve. Shortly after his arrival, however, he took a turn for the worse, and on February 22nd he wrote to Victor Seroff:

. . . I am ailing all the time. And I play fewer concerts than the number I cancel. Right now, I have cancelled three concerts so that I can go 'direkt' to California . . .

With his wife beside him, Rachmaninoff caught a slow train back to Los Angeles; a laborious and painful journey which took sixty hours. An ambulance was there to meet them, and took

131

Rachmaninoff immediately to the Hospital of the Good Samaritan. A series of tests did not at first disclose the nature of his illness. But cancer was suspected, and Natalia took him home to Elm Drive. His daughter and sister-in-law came from New York, and so did Fedya Chaliapin, the son of the bass. The presence of his family and the ministerings of a Russian nurse made his suffering more bearable. Further tests now revealed the terrible truth: Rachmaninoff was suffering from a rare and fast-spreading cancer.

A radio was installed in his room so that he could follow the news of the war. By March 1943 the American offensive was proving irresistible across the Pacific, and the German Army had been cleared out of North Africa. Cheered by this news, Rachmaninoff was encouraged by the advance of the Red Army, following the heroic Russian resistance to the German offensive at the seige of Stalingrad at the end of 1942. After Stalingrad, Midway and El Alamein, the Axis powers were fighting from a position of retreat on all fronts.

132

Comforted as he was by this news, in the last week of March Rachmaninoff's condition deteriorated: unable to eat, he passed into a coma on March 26th. The next day a cable arrived from Russia, signed by many Soviet composers, to congratulate him on his seventieth birthday, which was due on April 2nd, but his life was slipping away. Early the following morning, March 28th 1943, the struggle was over.

Index

Selective listing of references
Illustrations are indicated in bold type

ILLUSTRATIONS ADDED FOR EXPANDED EDITION

In creating this expanded edition, more than thirty illustrations have been added as unnumbered pages at various places within the text. Following is a key to those insertions.